HAL•LEONARD®

GUITAR
PLAY-ALONG

AUDIO
ACCESS
INCLUDED

VOL. 183

BUDDY GUY

PLAYBACK+
Speed • Pitch • Balance • Loop

To access audio visit:
www.halleonard.com/mylibrary

Enter Code
4452-7856-0133-5840

Cover photo: Photofest

ISBN 978-1-4950-0243-4

HAL•LEONARD®
CORPORATION
7777 W. BLUEMOUND RD. P.O. BOX 13819 MILWAUKEE, WI 53213

Visit Hal Leonard Online at
www.halleonard.com

CONTENTS

GUITAR NOTATION LEGEND

THE MUSICAL STAFF shows pitches and rhythms and is divided by bar lines into measures. Pitches are named after the first seven letters of the alphabet.

TABLATURE graphically represents the guitar fingerboard. Each horizontal line represents a string, and each number represents a fret.

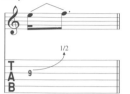
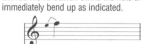

4th string, 2nd fret   1st & 2nd strings open, played together   open D chord

HALF-STEP BEND: Strike the note and bend up 1/2 step.

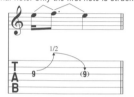

WHOLE-STEP BEND: Strike the note and bend up one step.

GRACE NOTE BEND: Strike the note and immediately bend up as indicated.

SLIGHT (MICROTONE) BEND: Strike the note and bend up 1/4 step.

BEND AND RELEASE: Strike the note and bend up as indicated, then release back to the original note. Only the first note is struck.

PRE-BEND: Bend the note as indicated, then strike it.

VIBRATO: The string is vibrated by rapidly bending and releasing the note with the fretting hand.

PALM MUTING: The note is partially muted by the pick hand lightly touching the string(s) just before the bridge.

HAMMER-ON: Strike the first (lower) note with one finger, then sound the higher note (on the same string) with another finger by fretting it without picking.

PULL-OFF: Place both fingers on the notes to be sounded. Strike the first note and without picking, pull the finger off to sound the second (lower) note.

LEGATO SLIDE: Strike the first note and then slide the same fret-hand finger up or down to the second note. The second note is not struck.

SHIFT SLIDE: Same as legato slide, except the second note is struck.

TRILL: Very rapidly alternate between the notes indicated by continuously hammering on and pulling off.

TAPPING: Hammer ("tap") the fret indicated with the pick-hand index or middle finger and pull off to the note fretted by the fret hand.

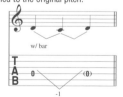

NATURAL HARMONIC: Strike the note while the fret-hand lightly touches the string directly over the fret indicated.

PINCH HARMONIC: The note is fretted normally and a harmonic is produced by adding the edge of the thumb or the tip of the index finger of the pick hand to the normal pick attack.

TREMOLO PICKING: The note is picked as rapidly and continuously as possible.

VIBRATO BAR DIVE AND RETURN: The pitch of the note or chord is dropped a specified number of steps (in rhythm), then returned to the original pitch.

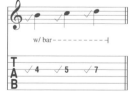

VIBRATO BAR SCOOP: Depress the bar just before striking the note, then quickly release the bar.

VIBRATO BAR DIP: Strike the note and then immediately drop a specified number of steps, then release back to the original pitch.

Additional Musical Definitions

(accent)   • Accentuate note (play it louder).

(staccato)   • Play the note short.

D.S. al Coda   • Go back to the sign (%), then play until the measure marked "*To Coda*," then skip to the section labelled "**Coda**."

D.C. al Fine   • Go back to the beginning of the song and play until the measure marked "*Fine*" (end).

Fill   • Label used to identify a brief melodic figure which is to be inserted into the arrangement.

N.C.   • Harmony is implied.

• Repeat measures between signs.

| 1. | 2. |

• When a repeated section has different endings, play the first ending only the first time and the second ending only the second time.

5

Damn Right, I've Got the Blues

Words and Music by Buddy Guy

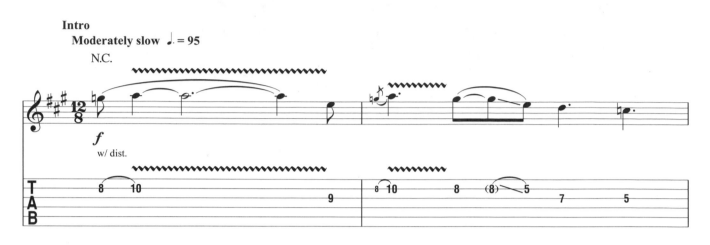

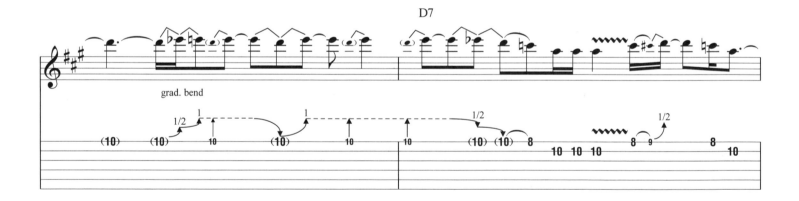

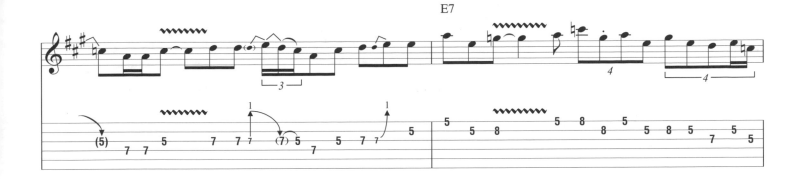

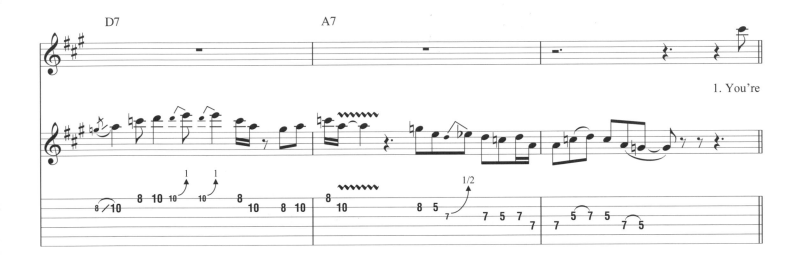

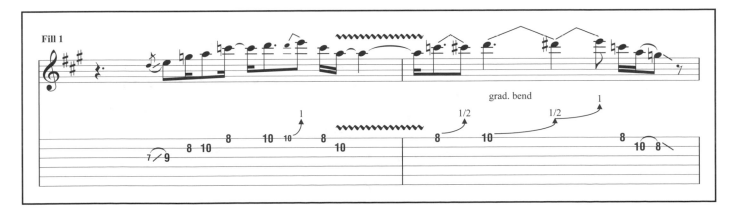

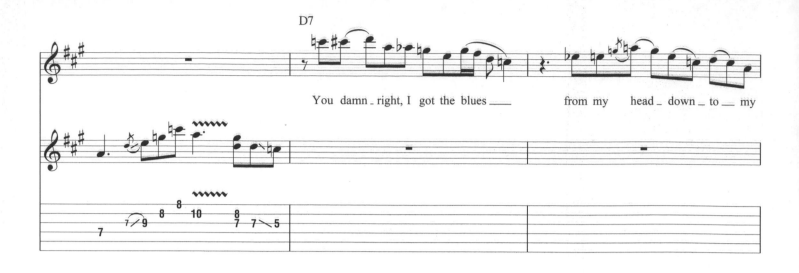

You damn _ right, I got the blues ___ from my head _ down _ to _ my

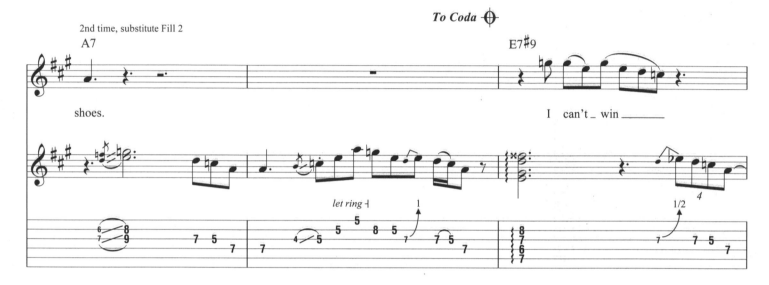

2nd time, substitute Fill 2

To Coda ⊕

shoes.

I can't _ win _____

'cause I don't have a thing _ to lose. __

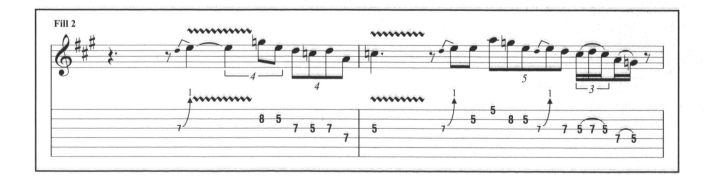

Verse

2. I stopped   by my daugh-ter's house. ＿   You know I just ＿want to use ＿ the phone. ＿

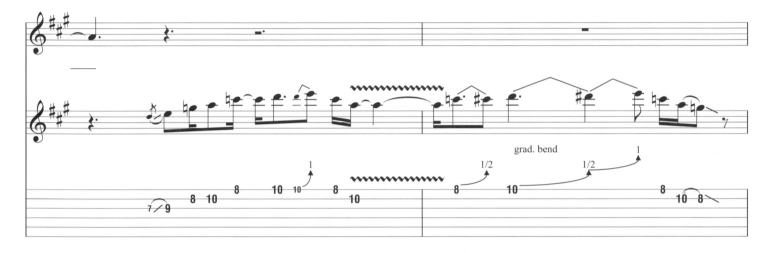

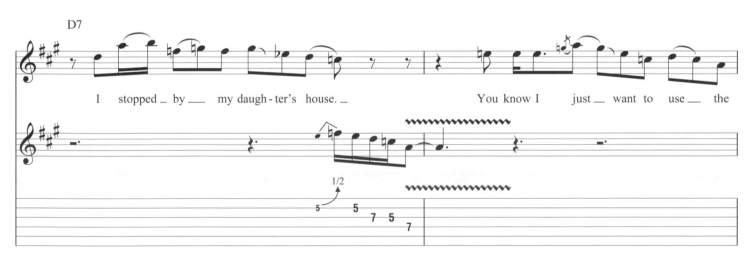

I   stopped ＿ by ＿ my daugh-ter's house. ＿   You know I   just ＿ want to use ＿ the

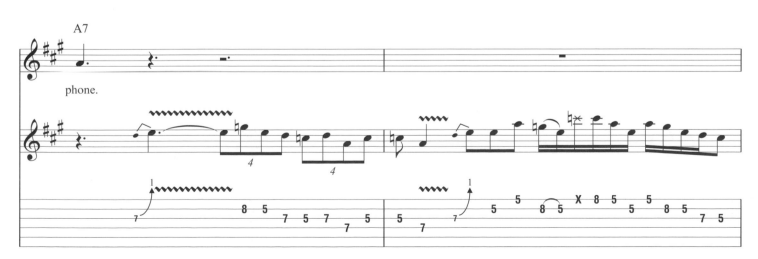

phone.

You know, my new grand-ba-by came to the door __ and say, "Grand-dad-dy, you know ain't no __

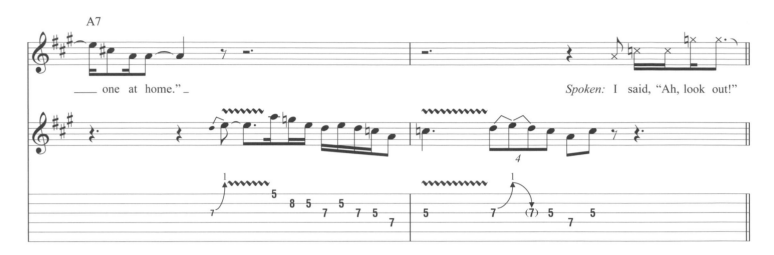

__ one at home." __

Spoken: I said, "Ah, look out!"

Guitar Solo

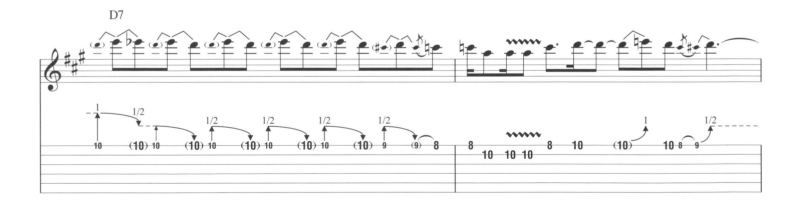

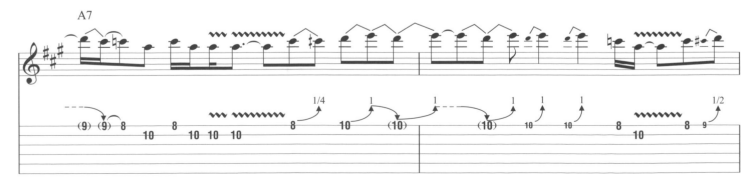

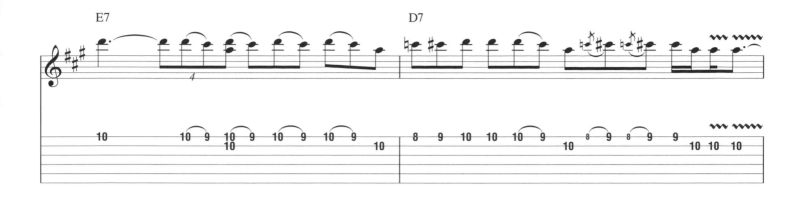

D.S. al Coda

⊕ Coda

You know I ___ can't win, ___ now peo - ple, ___ 'cause I don't have a thing ___ to

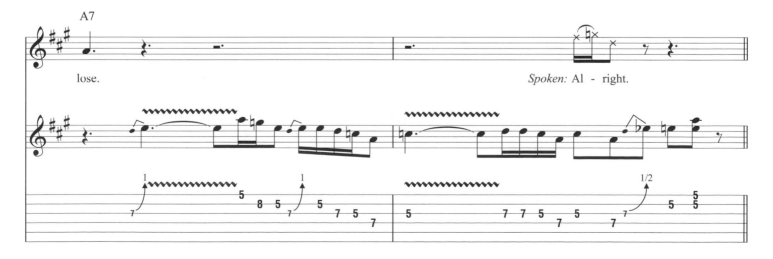

lose.

Spoken: Al - right.

Guitar Solo

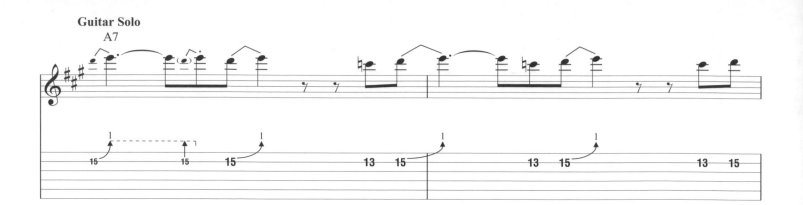

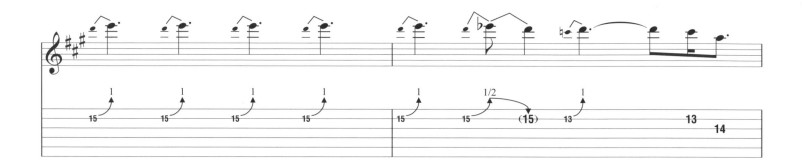

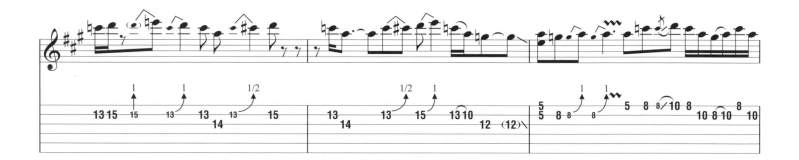

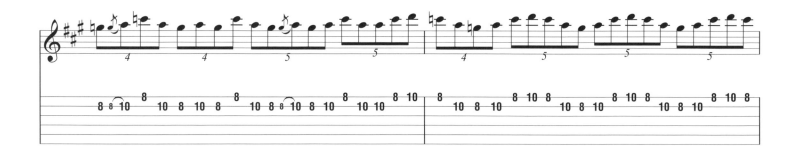

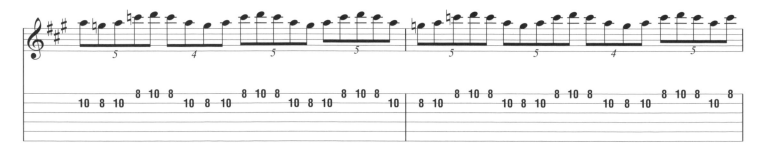

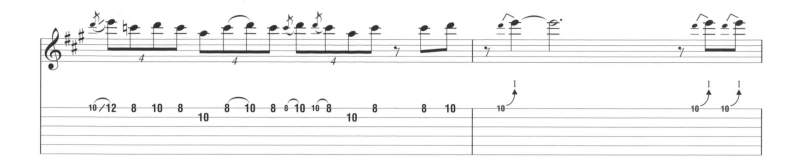

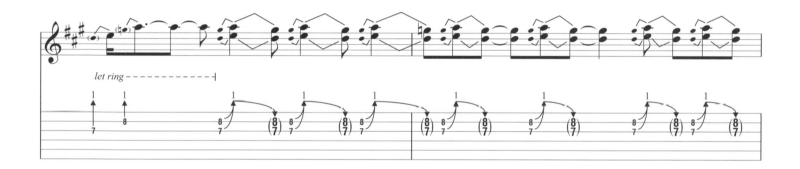

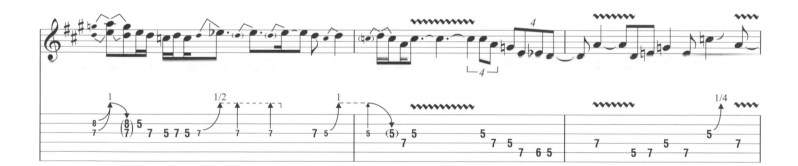

Outro

Gtr. tacet

A7

You damn ___ right, ___ I've got the blues. ___

You damn ___ right, ___ I've got the blues. ___

You damn ___ right, ___ I got the blues. ___

Spoken: Yeah. ___

Begin fade

w/ clean tone

Fade out

Midnight Train

Words and Music by Jon Tiven and Roger Reale

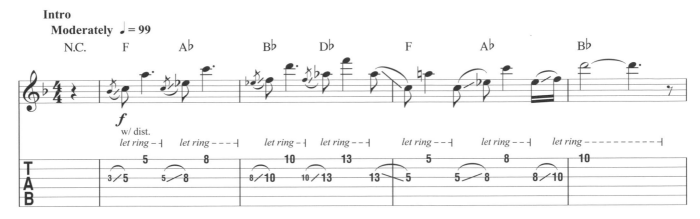

busi - ness, wait - in' for ___ that mid - night train. A, no -

bod - y in sight, ___ star - in' at ___ my shoes, _____ I took out my pa - per to

find me some _ good news, _____ mind - in' my own busi - ness

when the tick - et man calls ___ my name. _____ Yeah, yeah, ___ babe. There

Chorus

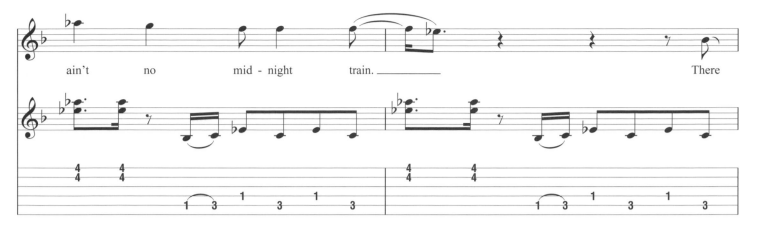

ain't   no   mid - night   train. _____   There

ain't   no   mid-night   train. _____   There   ain't   no   mid-night   train, __

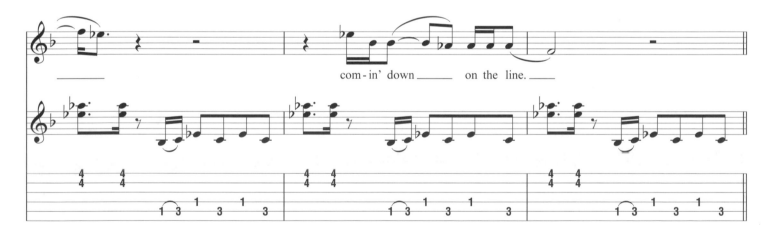

_____   com - in' down _____   on the line. _____

Interlude

N.C.

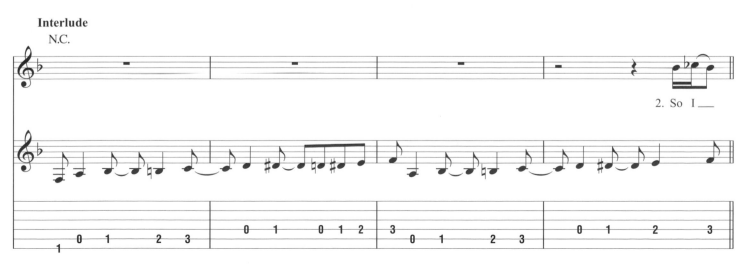

2. So I ___

Verse

say ___ ain't too much trou - ble, when's the lo - cal out of

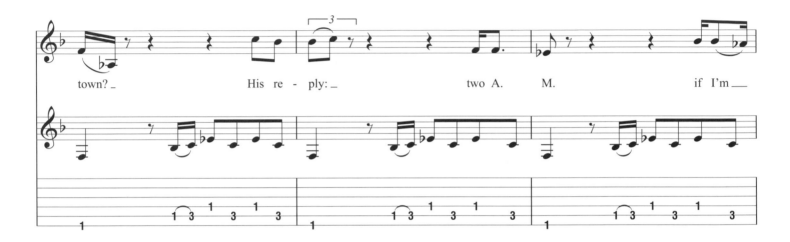

town? ___ His re - ply: ___ two A. M. if I'm ___

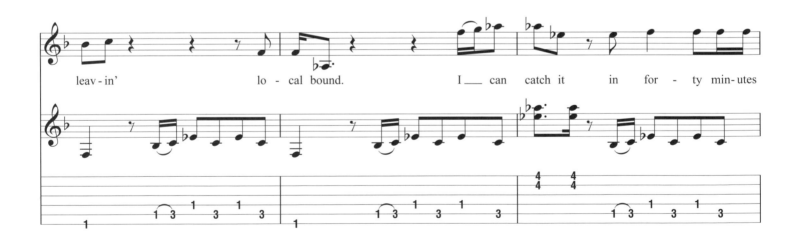

leav - in' lo - cal bound. I ___ can catch it in for - ty min - utes

if I want to grab the ex - press, _____ but the

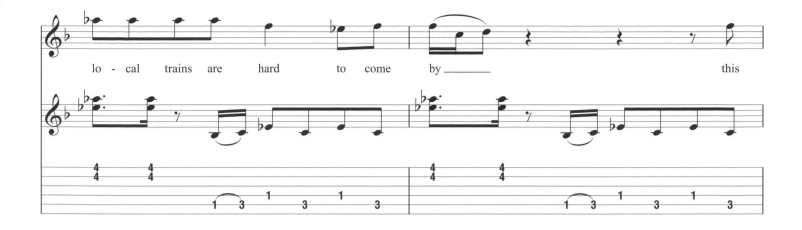

lo - cal trains are hard to come by _____ this

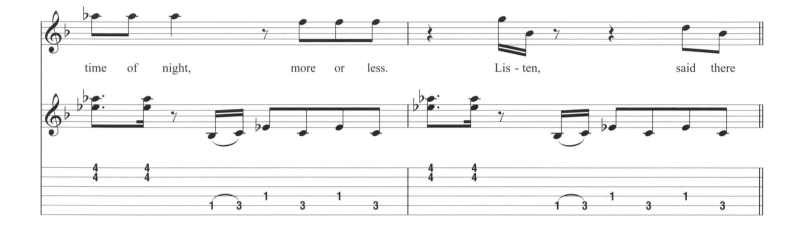

time of night, more or less. Lis - ten, said there

Chorus

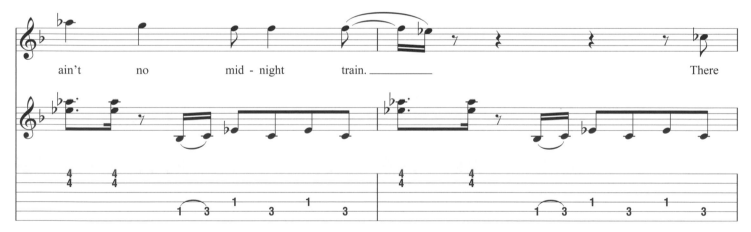

ain't no mid - night train. _____ There

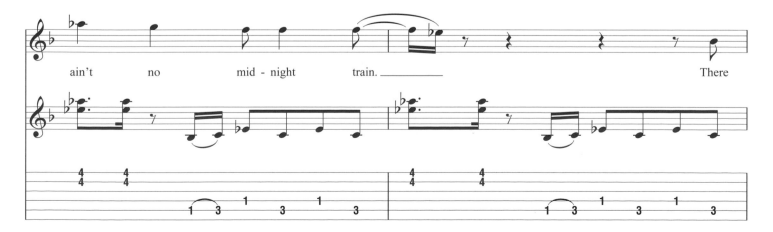

ain't no mid - night train. _____ There

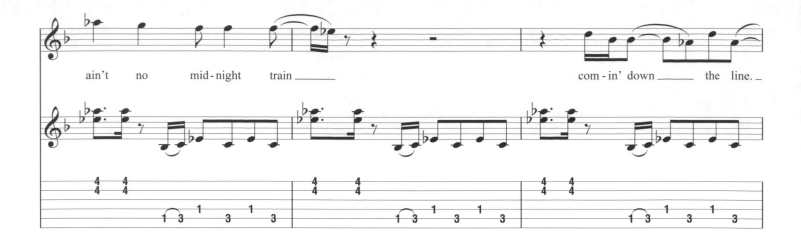

ain't no mid-night train _____   com-in' down _____ the line. __

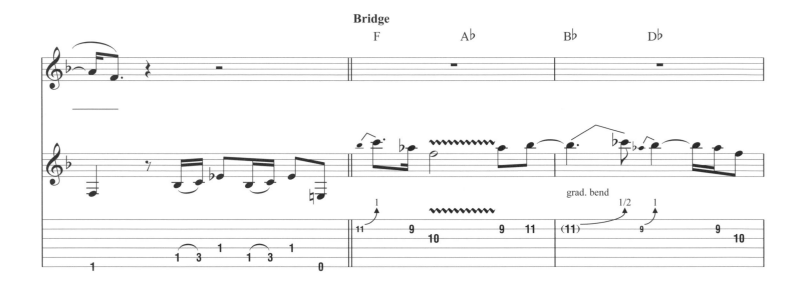

Bridge

F   Ab   Bb   Db

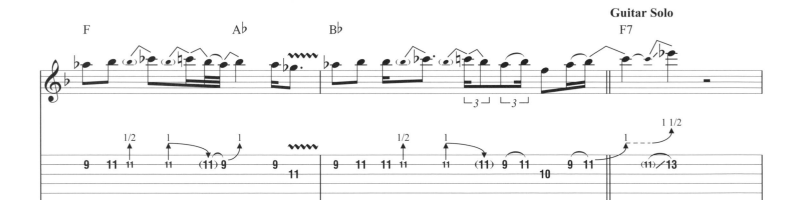

F   Ab   Bb   **Guitar Solo**

F7

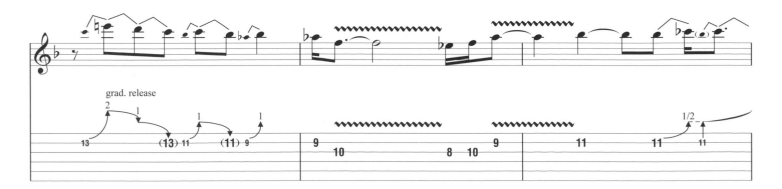

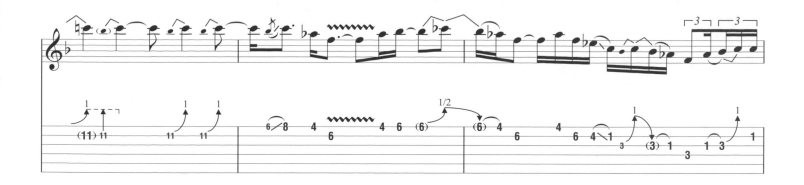

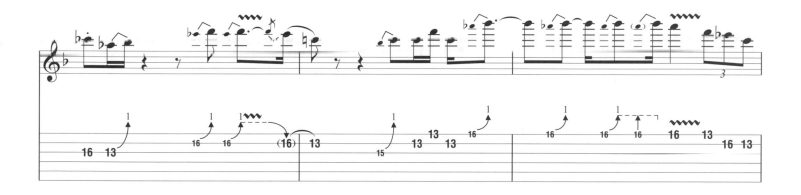

3. So I

Verse

stood ____ for for-ty min-utes, it was rain - in' and it was

cold. ___ When the ex - press rolled down the track I did-n't

(When the ex - press, a, rolled down the track I did not

Chorus

care where gon - na go. He said there ain't no mid-night train. ___

care where it was gon - na go. Yeah, yeah.)

_____ There ain't no mid-night train. _____ There

ain't no mid - night train, _____

com-in' down _____ the line. _

Guitar Solo

F7

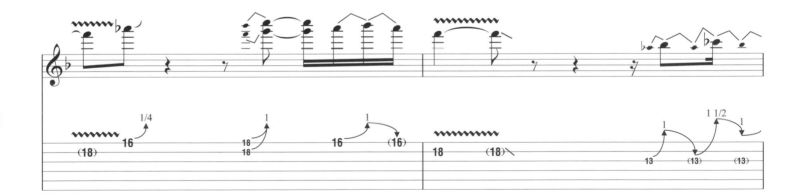

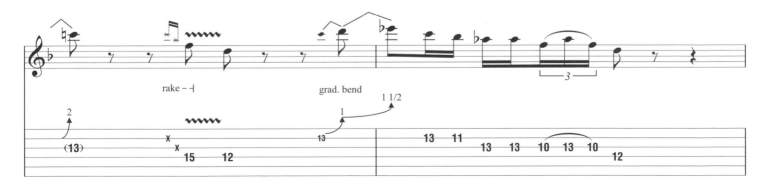

rake

grad. bend

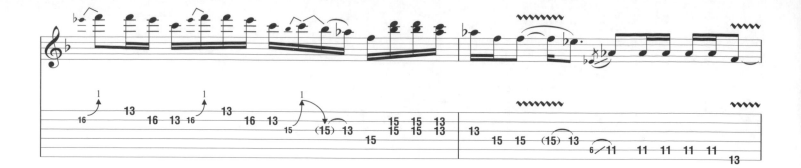

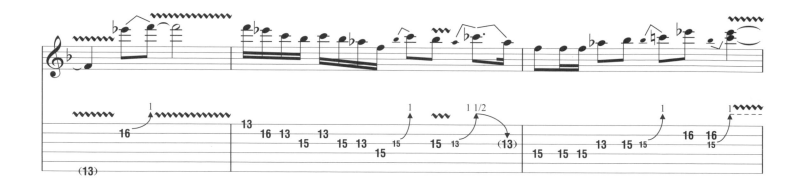

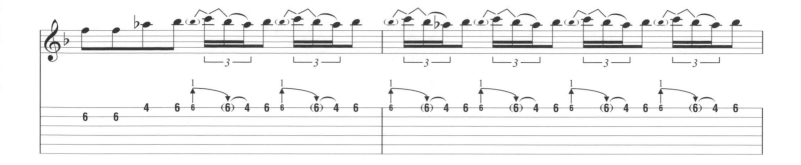

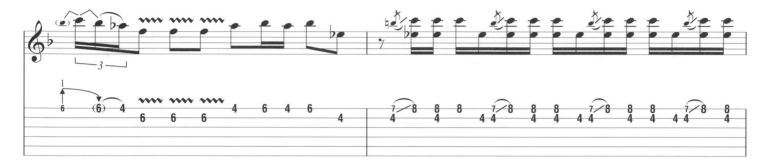

Begin fade

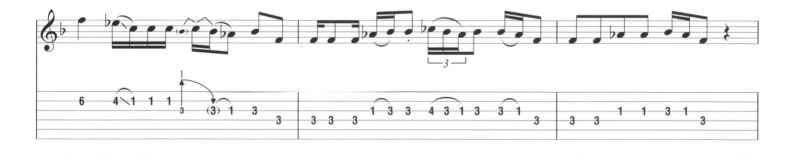

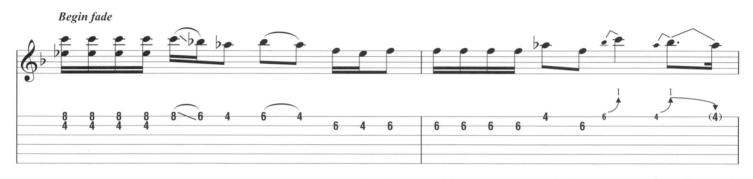

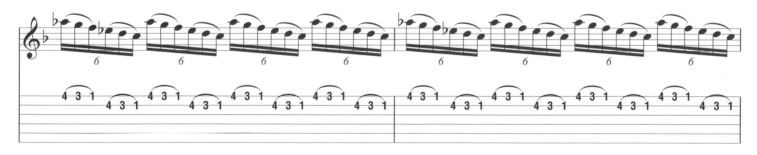

Fade out

Feels Like Rain

Words and Music by John Hiatt

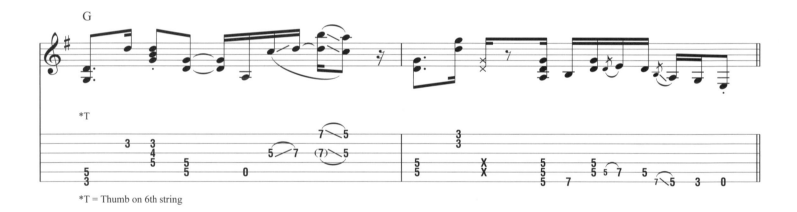

*T = Thumb on 6th string

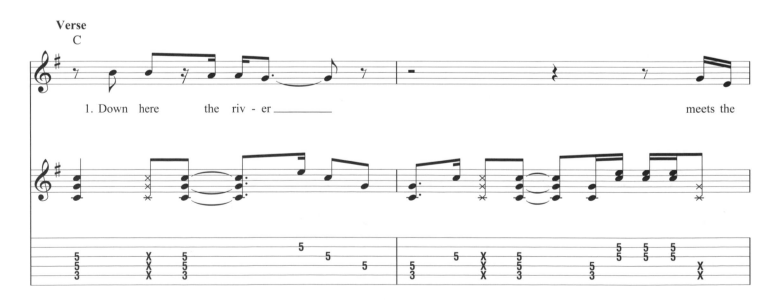

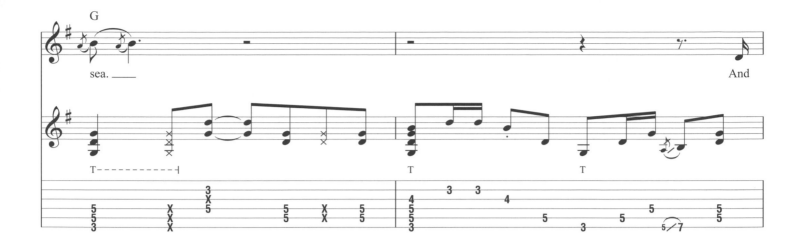

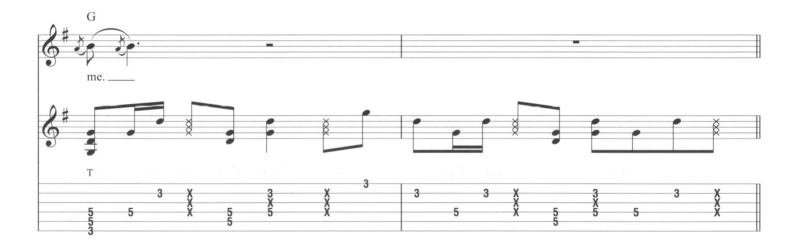

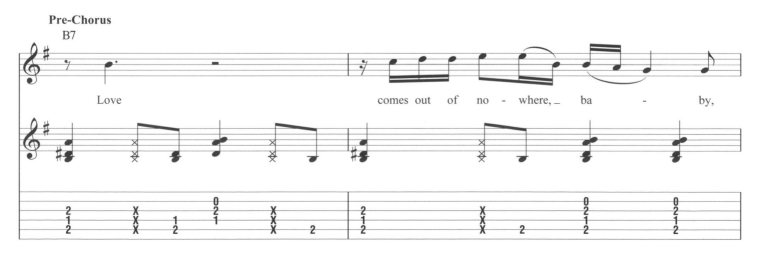

just like a hur - ri - cane. _____ And it feels like

Chorus

rain. _____ And it feels like, ah,

rain. _____

w/ pick & finger

Verse

2. Ly - ing here un - der - neath the stars _____ right next to

28

and the wind_ howls_ out your name._____ And it feels like

Chorus

rain. ___ And it feels like, ah,

w/ pick & finger

rain. _____

w/ pick & finger

Guitar Solo

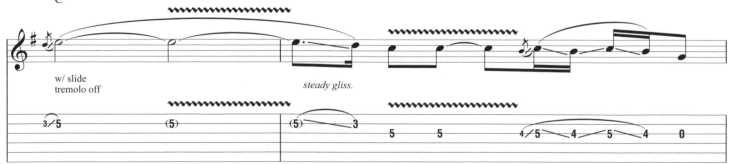

w/ slide
tremolo off   *steady gliss.*

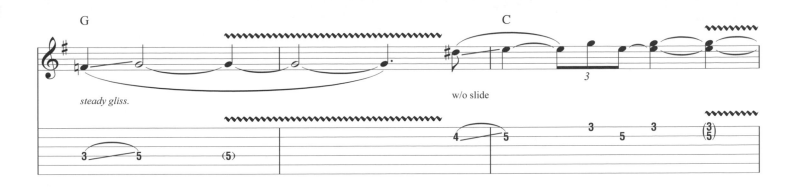

steady gliss.   w/o slide

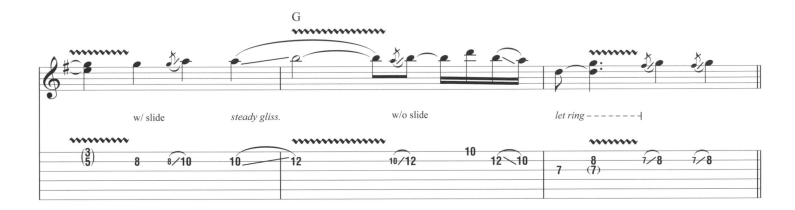

w/ slide   *steady gliss.*   w/o slide   *let ring --------*

Pre-Chorus

B7

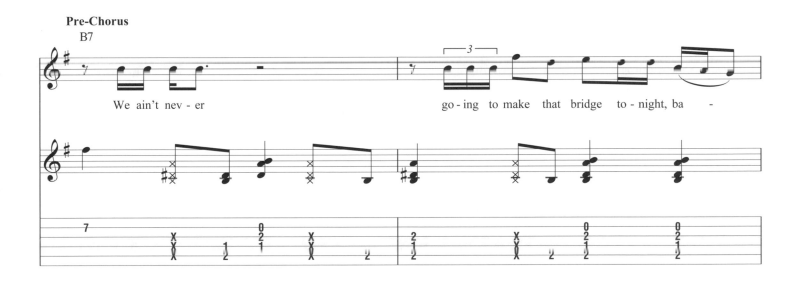

We ain't nev - er   go - ing to make that bridge to - night, ba -

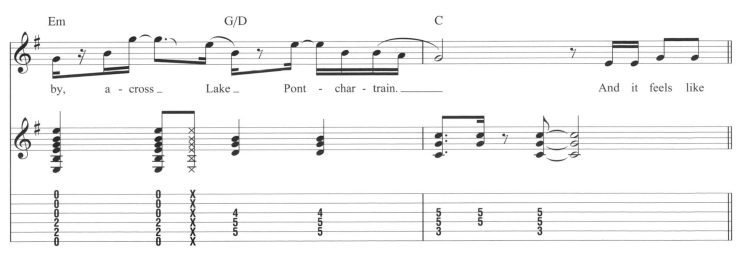

by,   a - cross Lake Pont - char - train.   And it feels like

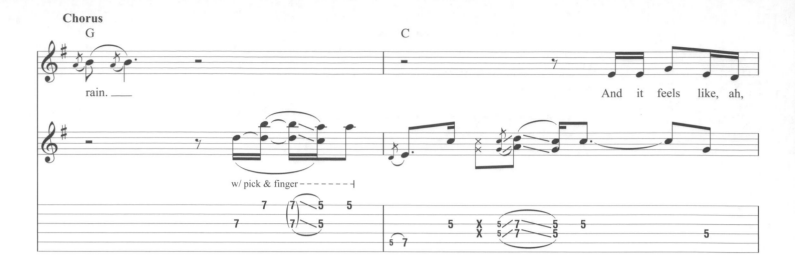

rain.

And it feels like, ah,

w/ pick & finger

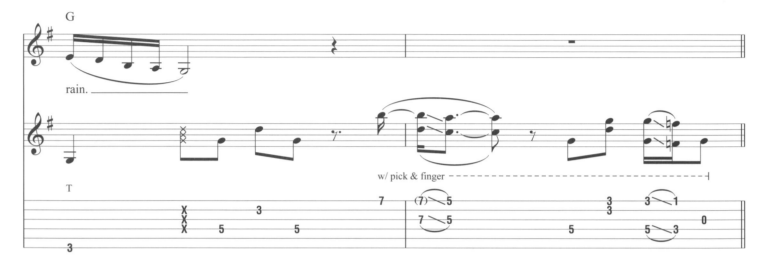

rain.

w/ pick & finger

Verse

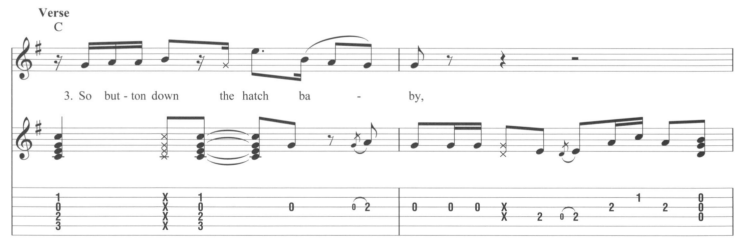

3. So but-ton down the hatch ba - by,

and leave your heart up your sleeve.

w/ pick & finger

P.M.

It looks like we're in _____ for storm-y weath-er. _____

That ain't no cause _____ for us to leave. _____

Pre-Chorus

Just lie here _____ in my arms. _____

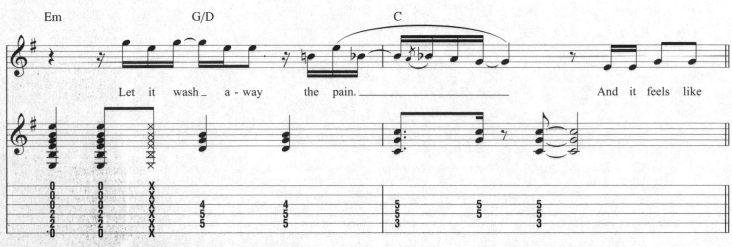

Let it wash _ a - way the pain. _____ And it feels like

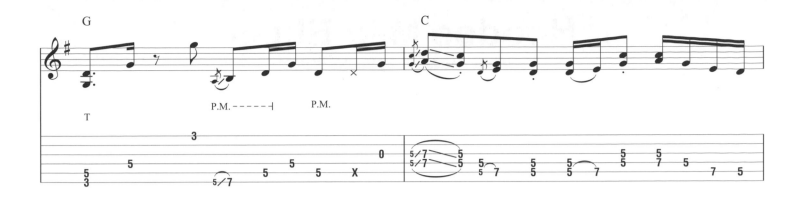

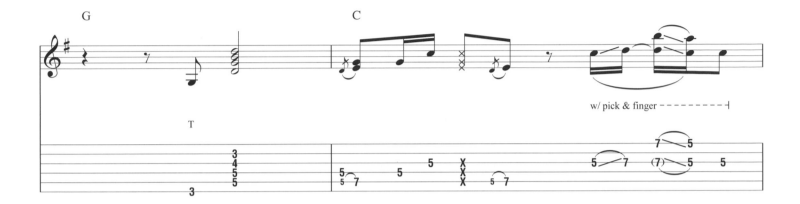

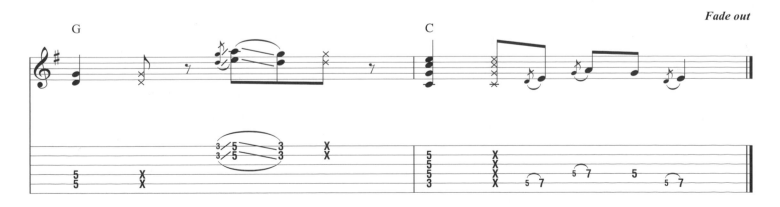

Hoodoo Man Blues

Words and Music by Junior Wells

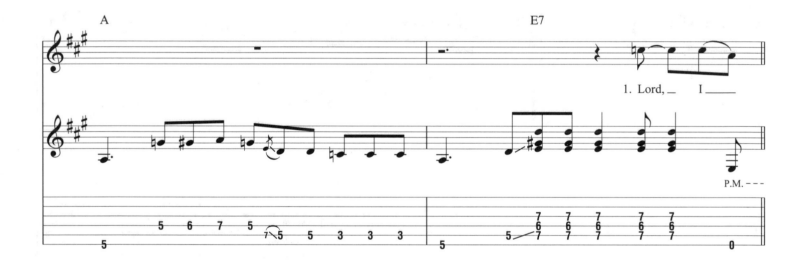

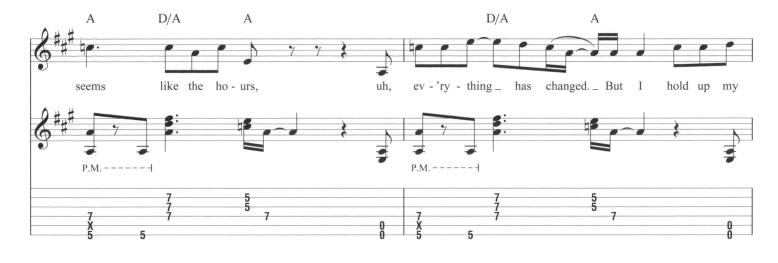

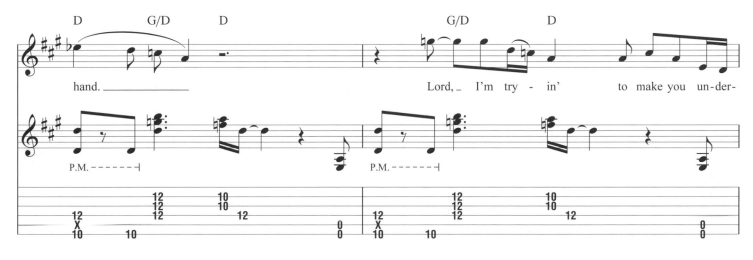

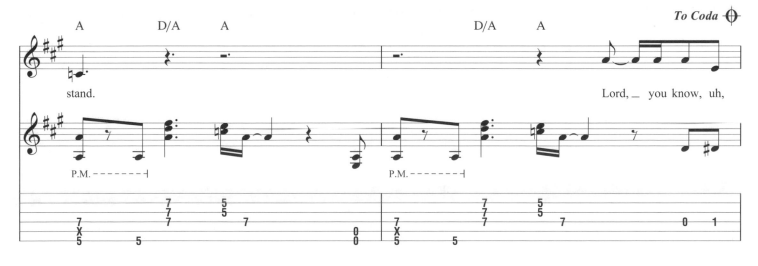

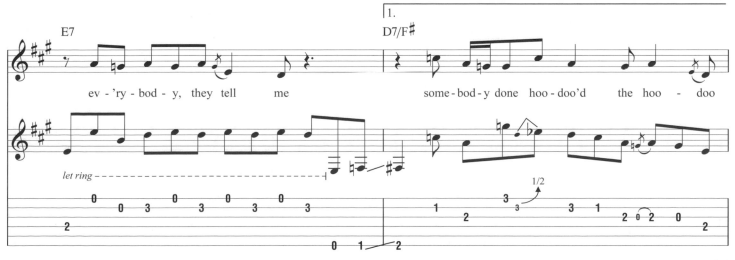

man.

2. Now, you know I,

that some-bod-y done hoo-doo'd the hoo-doo man. *Ha, ha, ha, ha, ha. Looky here, baby.*

Harmonica Solo

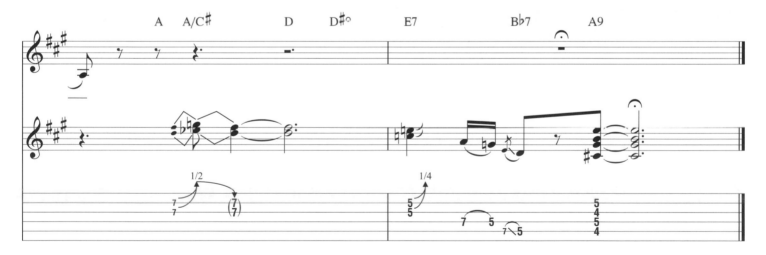

Additional Lyrics

2. Now, you know I, I buzzed your bell this mornin', baby,
   You had your elevator runnin' slow.
   I buzzed your bell, little girl, to take me up on the, uh, third floor.
   But I hold up my hand.
   Lord, I'm tryin' to make you understand.
   Lord, you know, uh, they tells the baby,
   That somebody done hoodoo'd the hoodoo man.
   Ha, ha, ha, ha, ha. Looky here, baby!

3. I say I'm gon', I tell you this time, babe,
   And I ain't gonna tell you no more
   That next time I tell you, might have to, uh, let you go.
   But I hold up my hand.
   Lord, I'm tryin' to make her understand.
   Lord, you know, ev'rybody they tell me
   Somebody done hoodoo'd the hoodoo man.

Man of Many Words

Words and Music by Buddy Guy

1. I don't care _ what no - bod - y say, I'm a man of a man-y word, _
2. *See additional lyrics*

I can speak things _ to your dar - lin' my dear, _ I could swear that you nev - er heard.

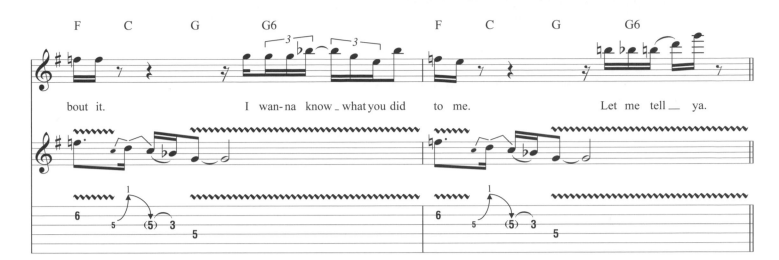

bout it.   I wan-na know _ what you did   to me.   Let me tell _ ya.

Guitar Solo

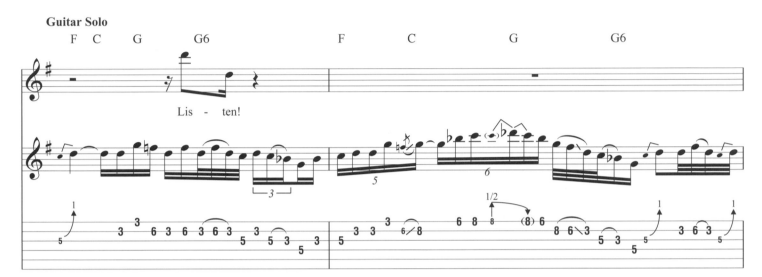

Lis - ten!

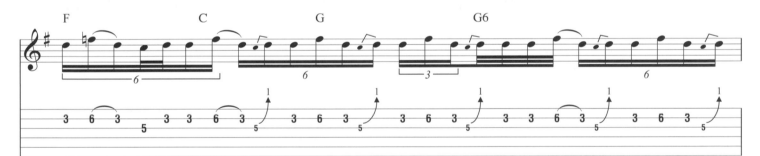

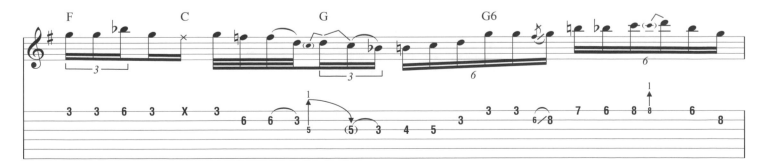

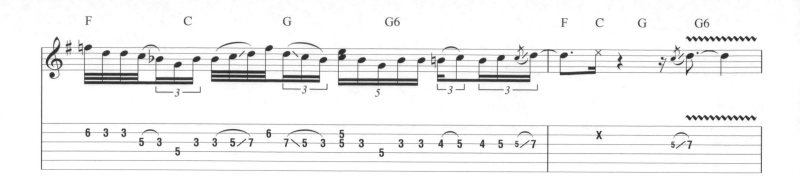

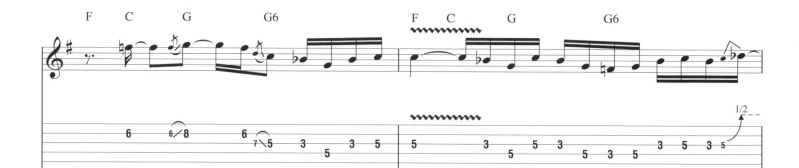

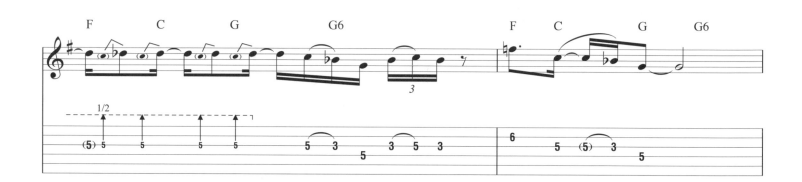

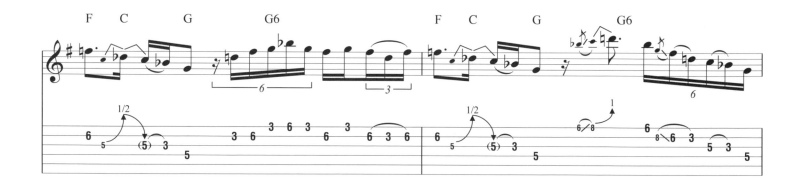

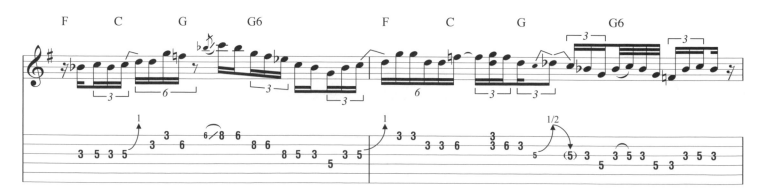

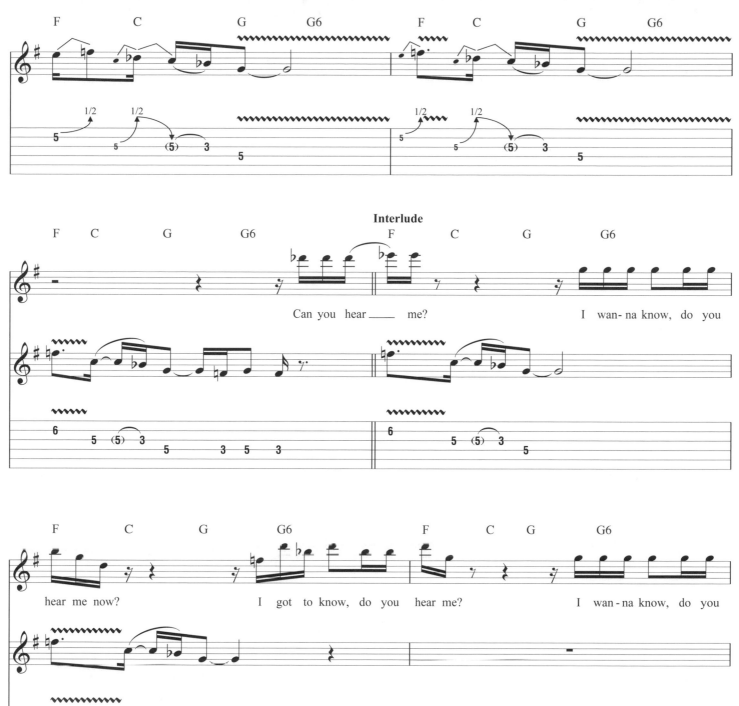

Interlude

Can you hear _____ me? I wan-na know, do you

hear me now? I got to know, do you hear me? I wan-na know, do you

hear? Oh! _____ Oh! _____

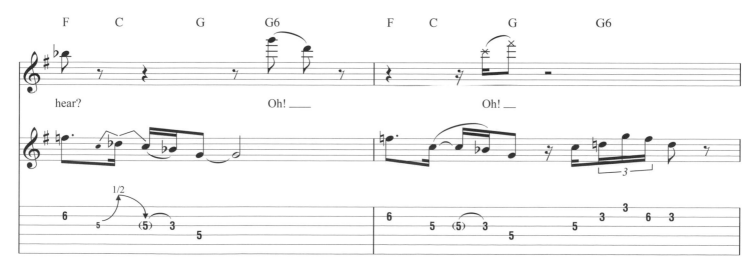

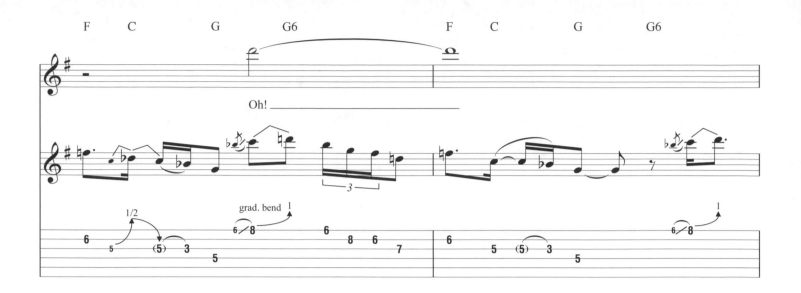

Oh! _____

Outro-Guitar Solo

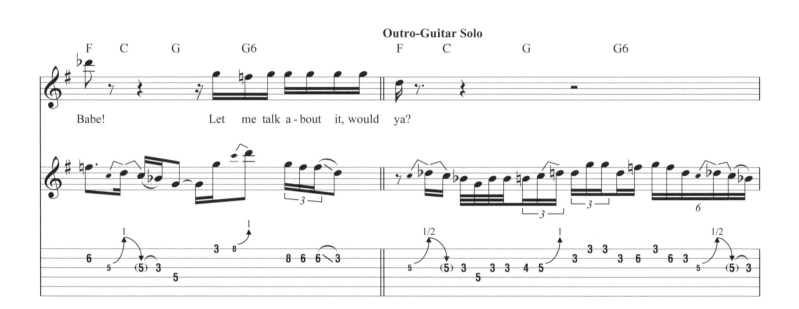

Babe!   Let   me talk a - bout   it, would   ya?

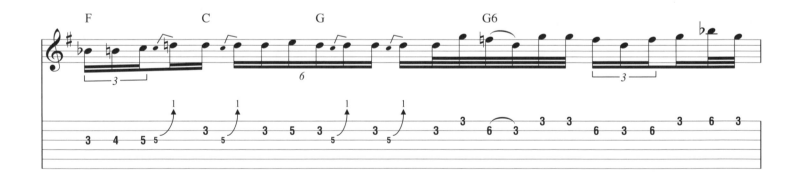

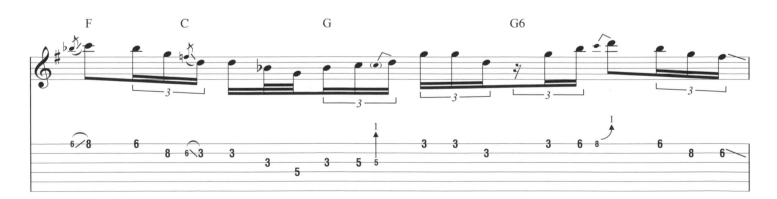

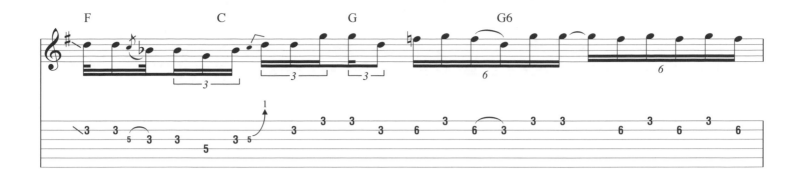

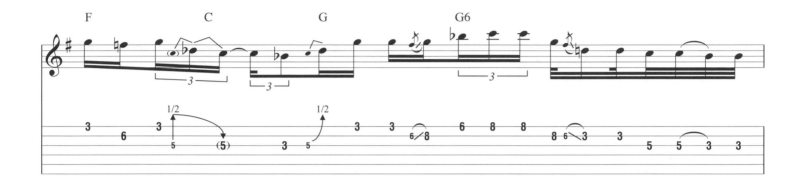

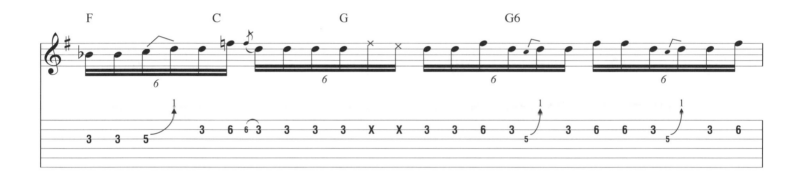

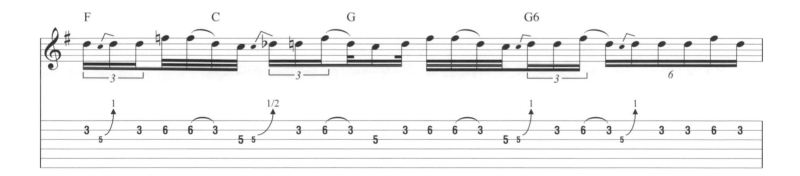

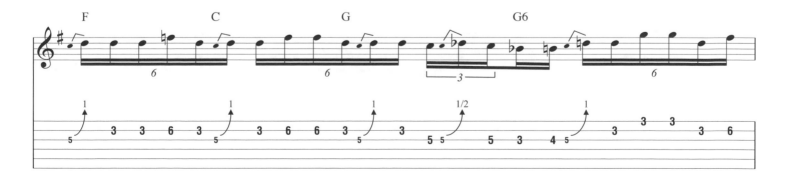

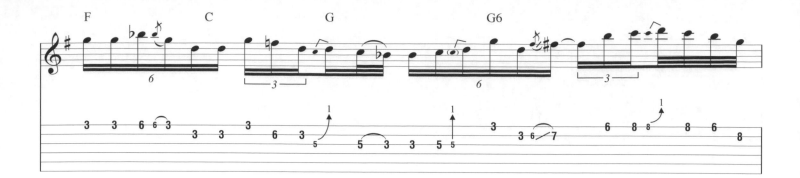

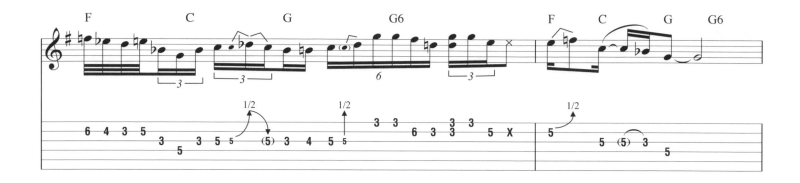

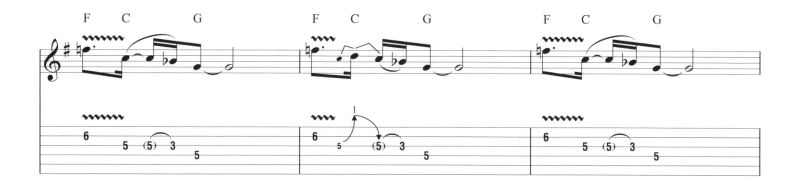

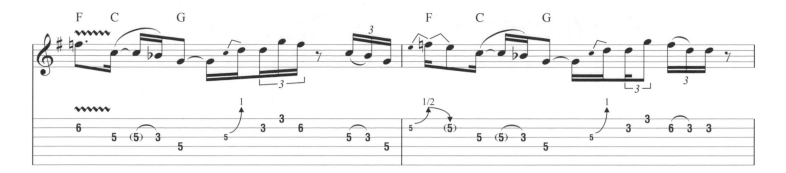

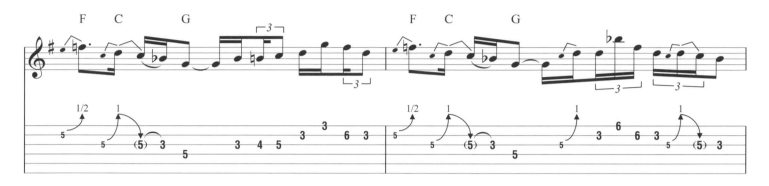

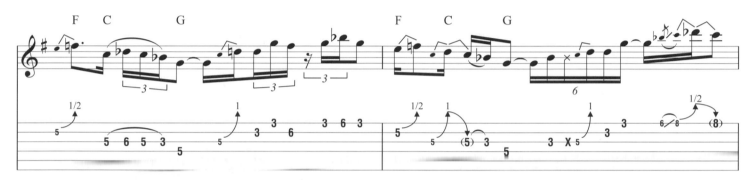

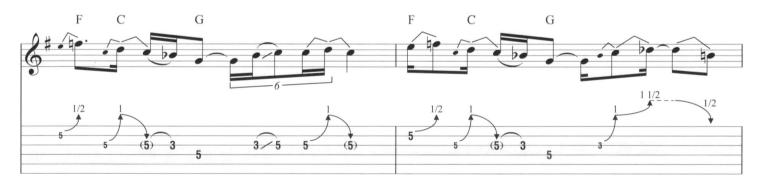

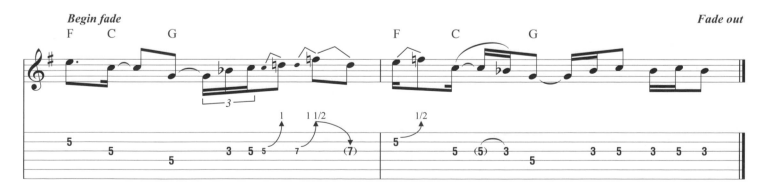

Additional Lyrics

2. When I rap my game and call your name, you will never be the same.
   In the midnight hours when you dream, my darlin', I swear you will call my name.
   I rap strong and I know I rap long,
   Come on, mama, let me turn you on, now come on.

Someone Else Is Steppin' In

Words and Music by Dennis LaSalle

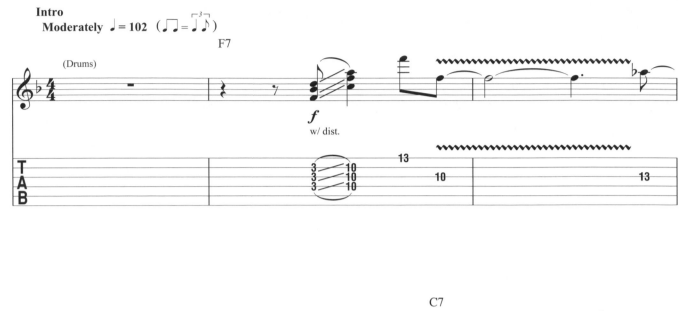

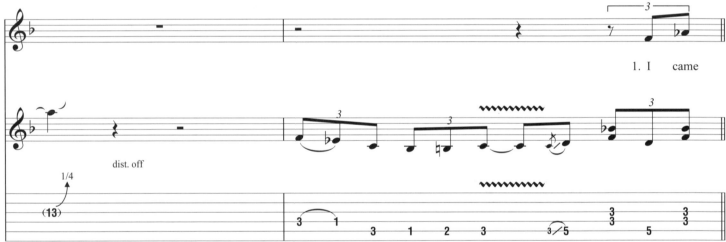

found out my key _____ no long - er fit my lock. _____ But, oh, _____

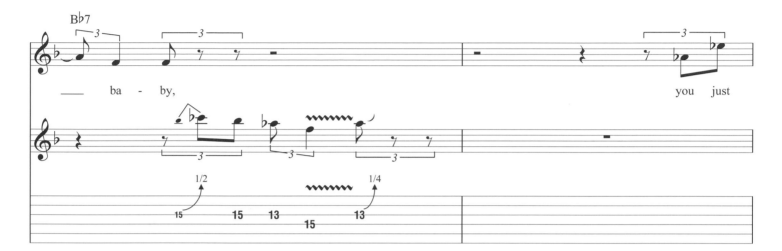

B♭7

_____ ba - by, _____ you just

F7

go right back out there _____ where you been. _____ But while _____

C9   B♭9

_____ you were slip - pin' out, _____   oh, _____ some - one else _____ was slip - pin'

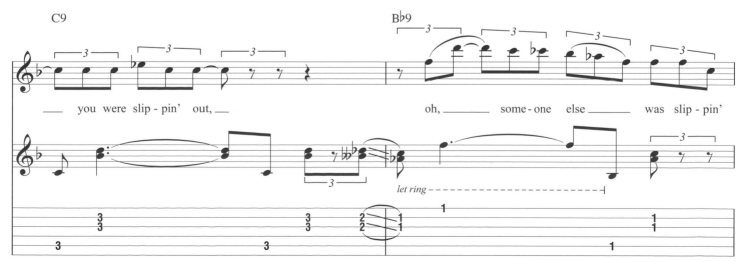

let ring -

Verse

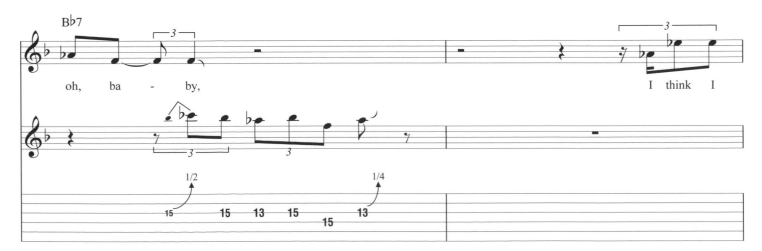

found my - self _____ a new friend. _____ But while ___

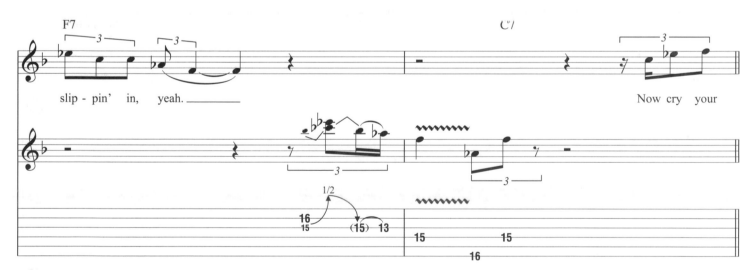

___ you were slip - pin' out, ___ ah, oh, ___ oh, _____ some - one else ___ was

slip - pin' in, yeah. _____ Now cry your

𝄋 Bridge

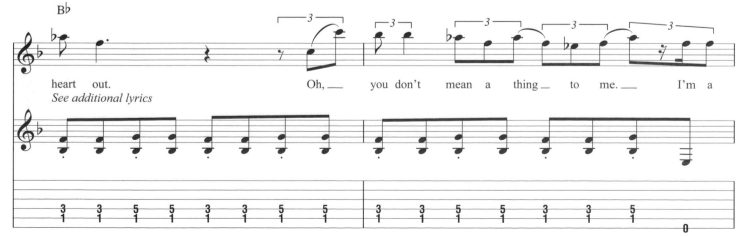

heart out. *See additional lyrics* Oh, ___ you don't mean a thing ___ to me. ___ I'm a

in. _____   Oh, Lord.

Guitar Solo

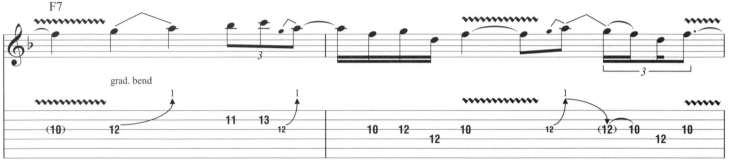

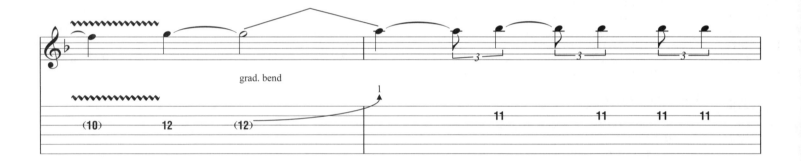

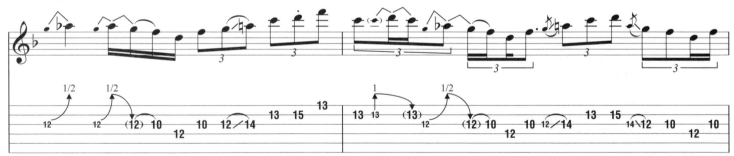

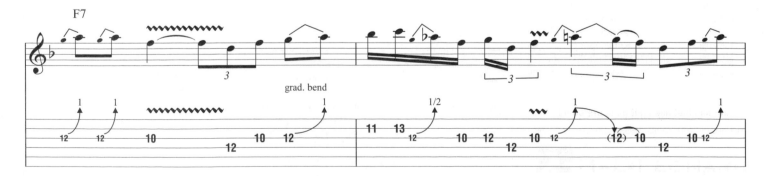

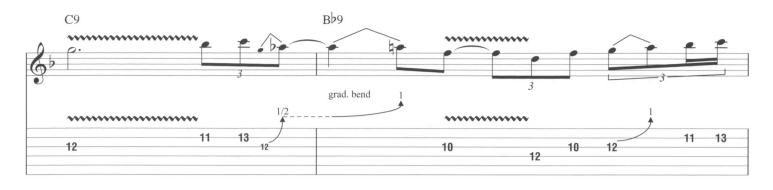

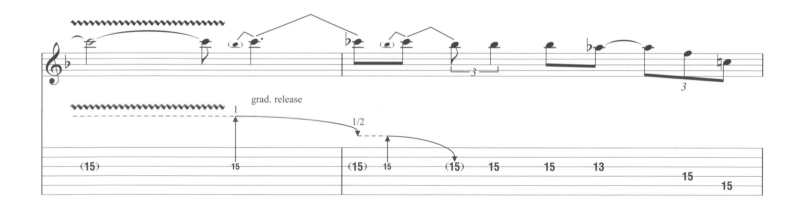

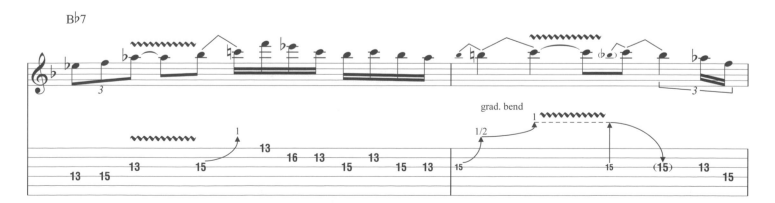

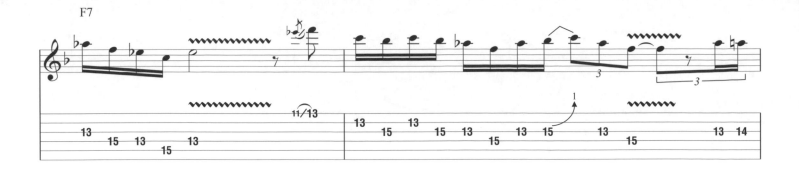

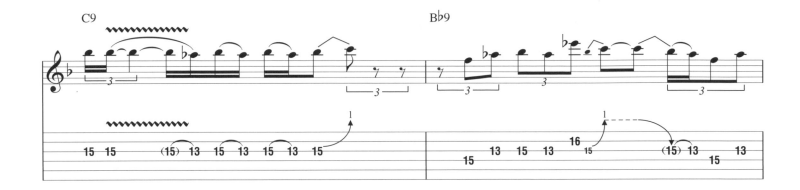

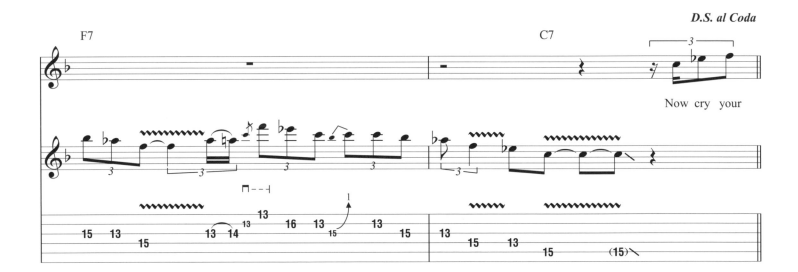

Now cry your

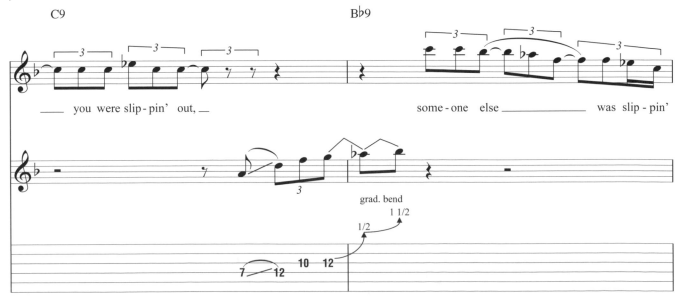

you were slip-pin' out, ___   some-one   else ___ was slip-pin'

grad. bend
1 1/2

1/2

Additional Lyrics

Bridge Now cry your heart out. Oh, you don't mean a thing to me.
I'm a brand-new man, even Stevie Wonder can see.
A new way to walk, people, and of wearin' my hair.
This big smile on my face, baby, you didn't put it there.

Stone Crazy

By Buddy Guy

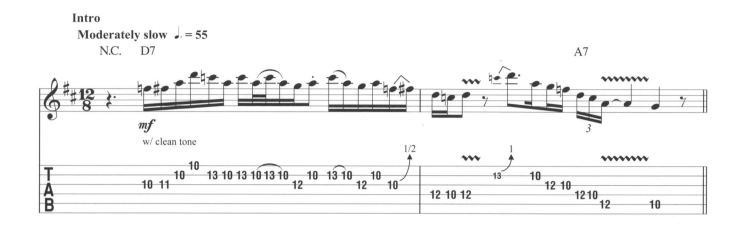

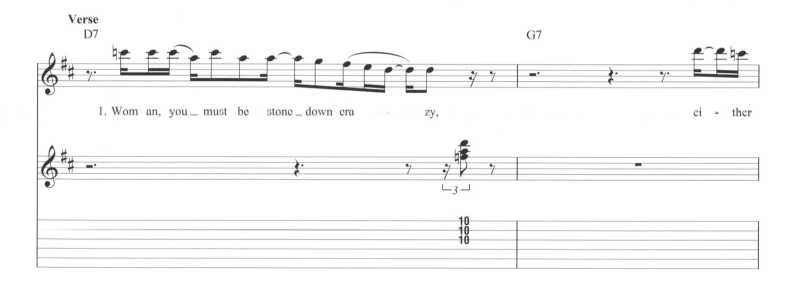

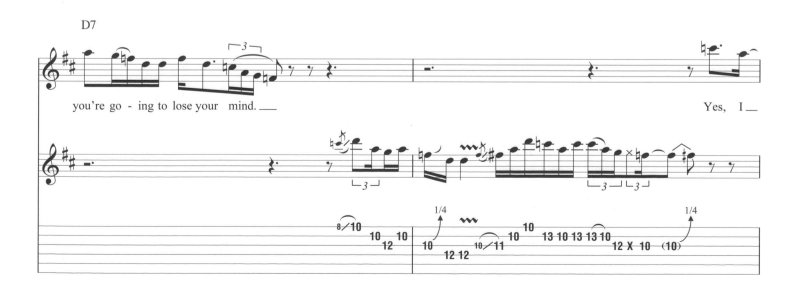

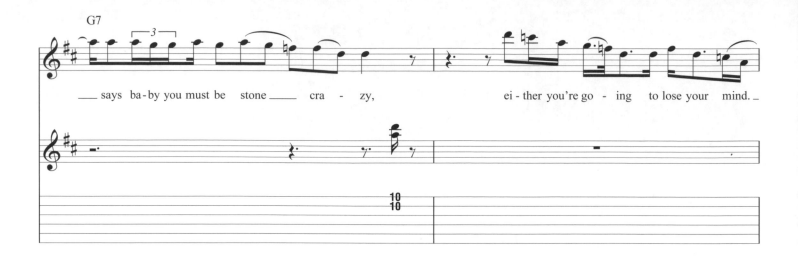

says ba-by you must be stone ___ cra - zy, ei - ther you're go - ing to lose your mind. ___

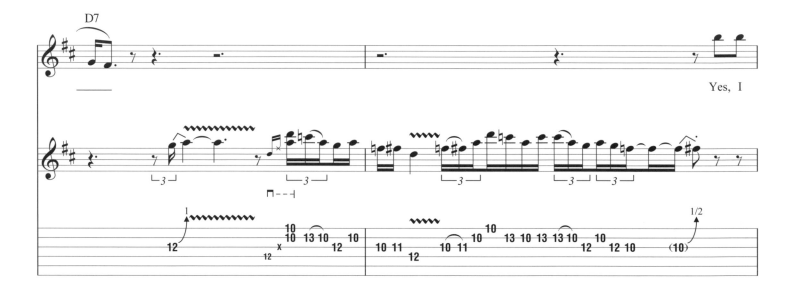

___ Yes, I

wan - na know how could you treat me so dirt - y, ba - by.

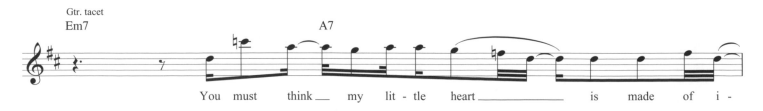

Gtr. tacet

You must think ___ my lit - tle heart ___ is made of i -

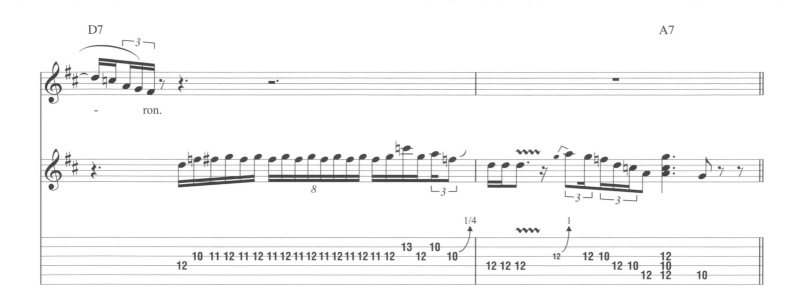

Verse

2. Lord, as I ____ sit here in my dark room, ____ tears roll-ing down _____ from my ____

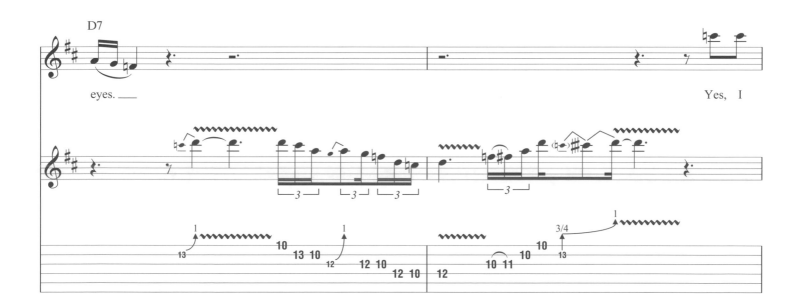

eyes. ____   Yes, I

says I sit here in my dark _____ room, ____ tears roll-ing all down _____ from my eyes. ____

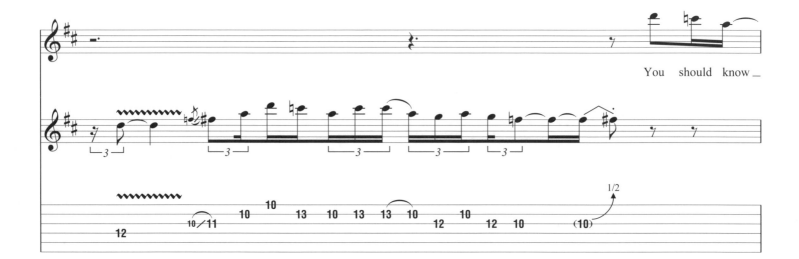

You should know __

__ my lit - tle ba - by looked at me and said, ___ "Dad - dy,

Gtr. tacet

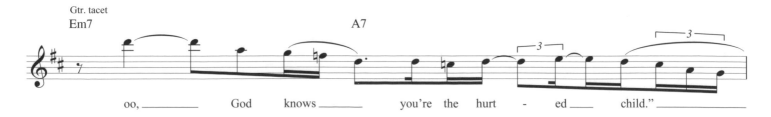

oo, ___ God knows ___ you're the hurt - ed ___ child." ___

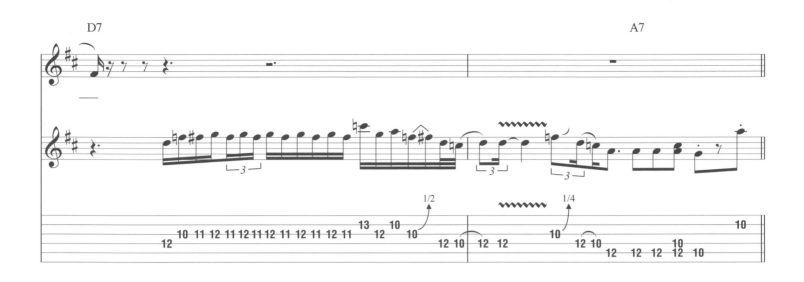

Guitar Solo

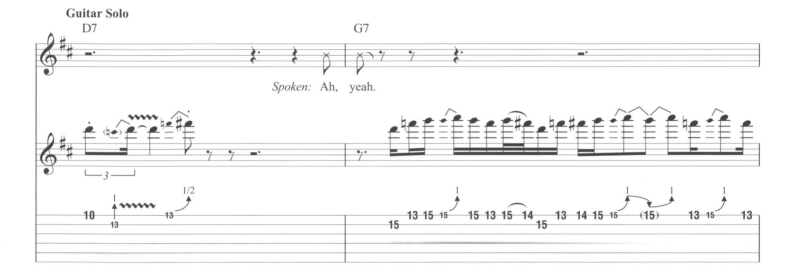

Spoken: Ah, yeah.

Some-bod-y come and get me.

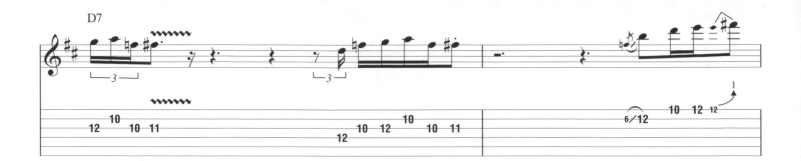

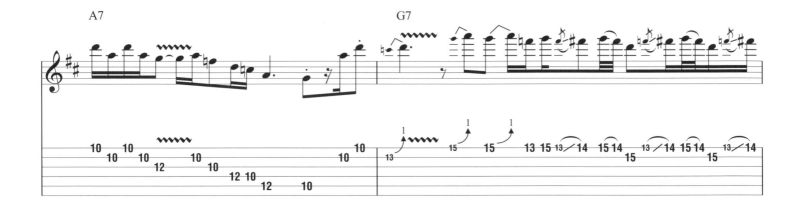

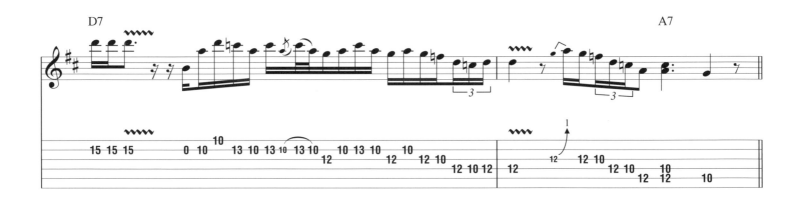

Verse

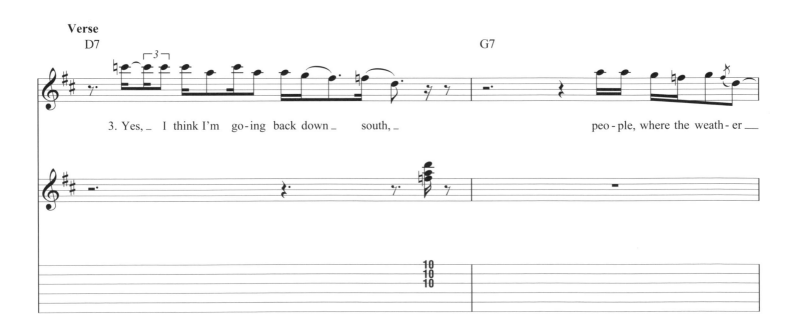

3. Yes, __ I think I'm go-ing back down __ south, __ peo-ple, where the weath-er __

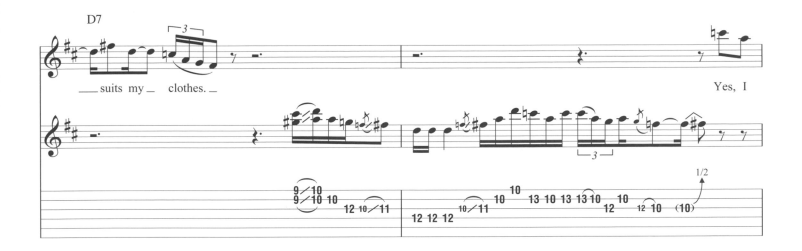

suits my clothes. Yes, I

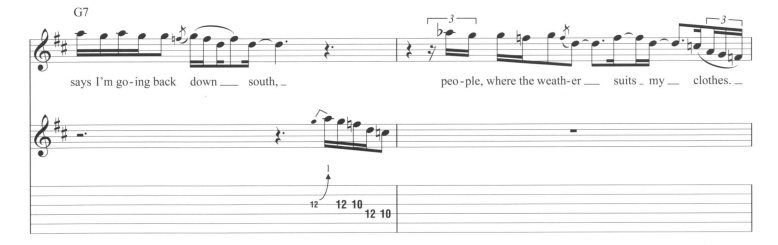

says I'm go-ing back down south, peo-ple, where the weath-er suits my clothes.

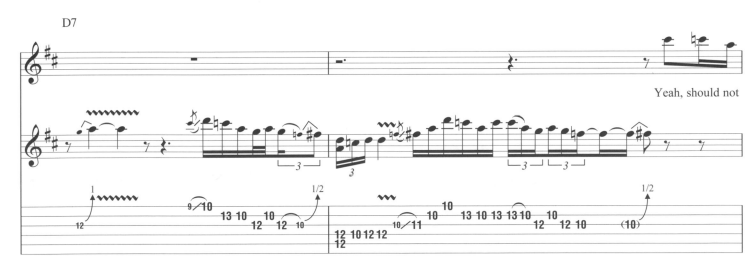

Yeah, should not

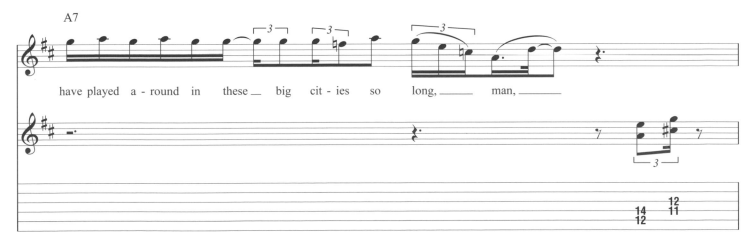

have played a-round in these big cit-ies so long, man,

oo, _____ till I al - most _____ just done froze. _____

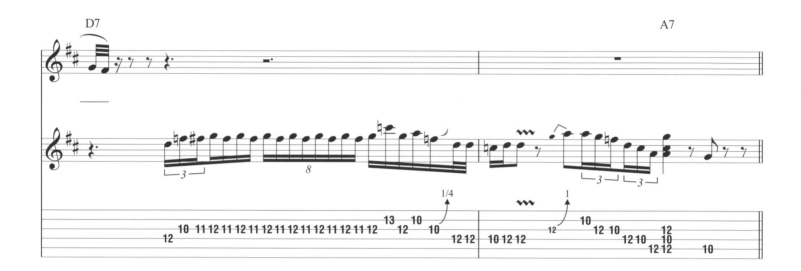

Verse
Gtr. tacet

4. Dar-ling, you must be stone cra - zy   or ei-ther you go - ing to lose your mind. _____

Yes, I

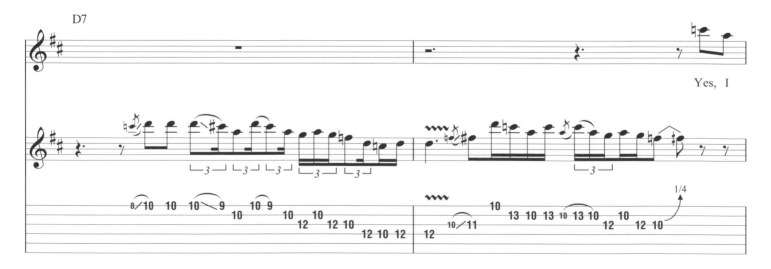

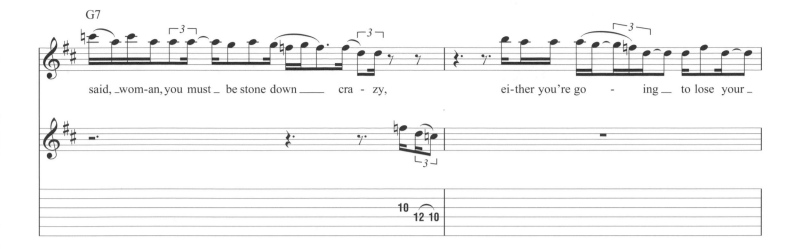

said, _wom-an, you must _ be stone down ____ cra - zy,   ei-ther you're go - ing __ to lose your _

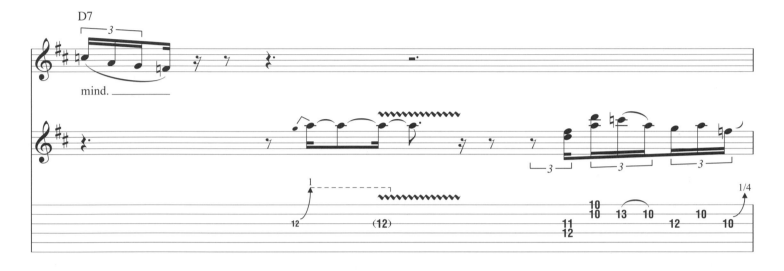

mind. ____

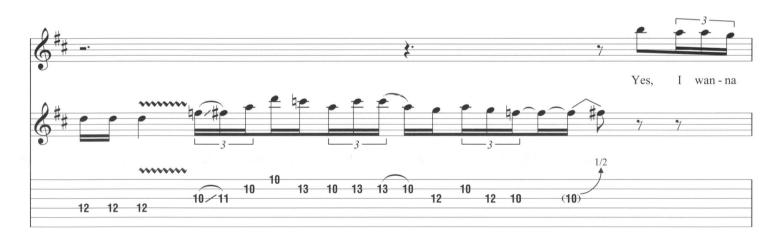

Yes,   I   wan - na

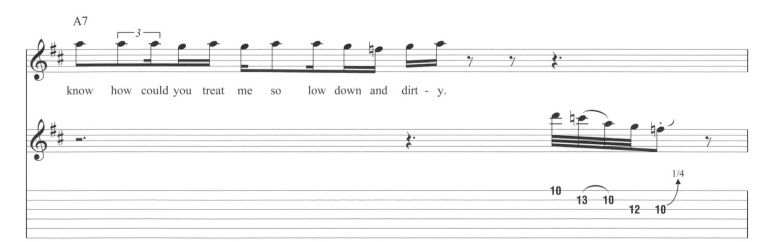

know   how   could you treat   me   so   low down and dirt - y.

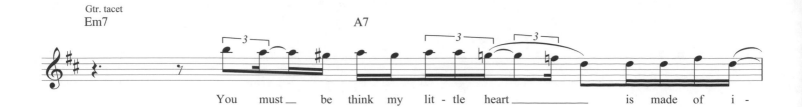

You must __ be think my lit - tle heart _____ is made of i -

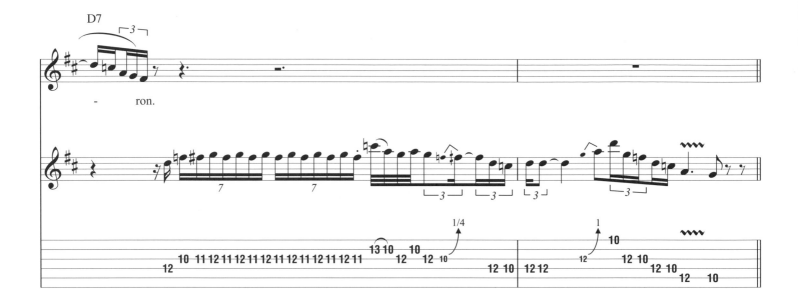

- ron.

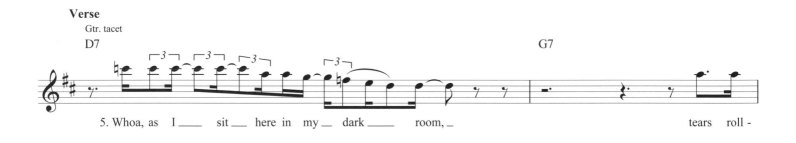

Verse

Gtr. tacet

5. Whoa, as I ____ sit ____ here in my __ dark ____ room, _ tears roll -

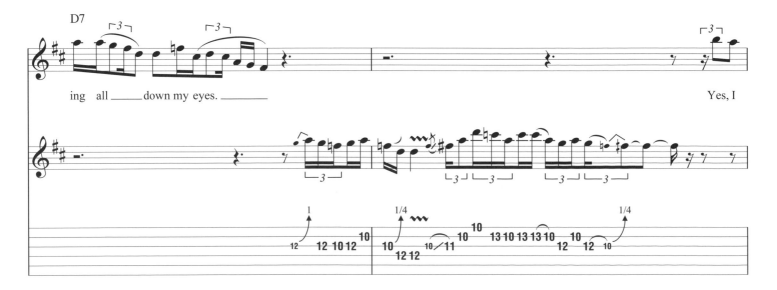

ing all ____ down my eyes. _____ Yes, I

says I sit right here, ___ right here in my dark ___ room,

tears roll - ing all _____ down _____ from my eyes. _____

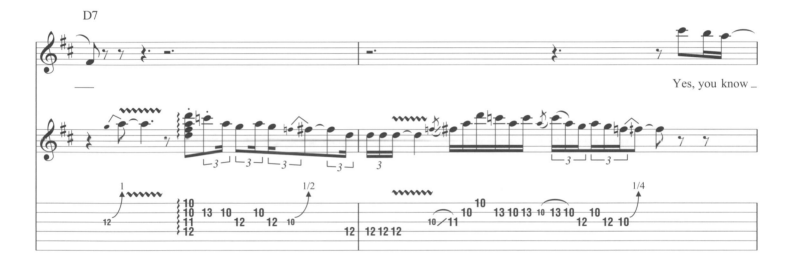

Yes, you know ___

___ my lit - tle girl ___ looked at me and ___ said, _____

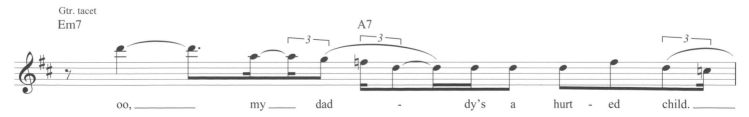

oo, _____ my ___ dad - dy's a hurt - ed child. _____

71

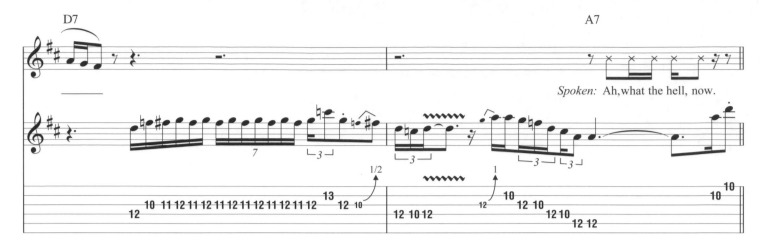

Spoken: Ah, what the hell, now.

Guitar Solo

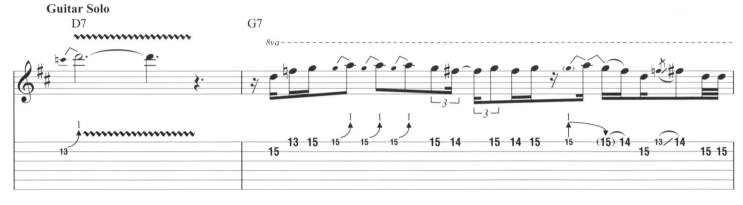

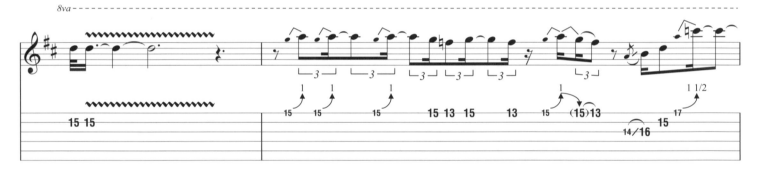

Spoken: Some-bod-y cut me, I 'spect.

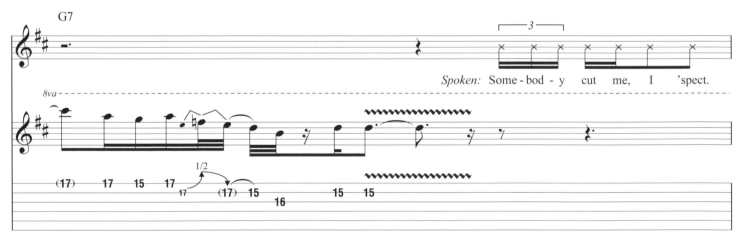

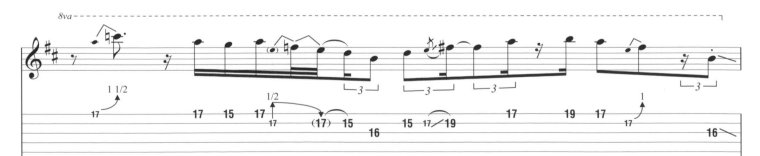

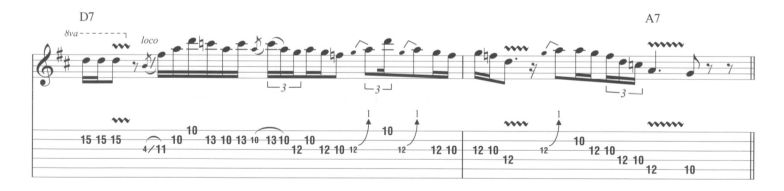

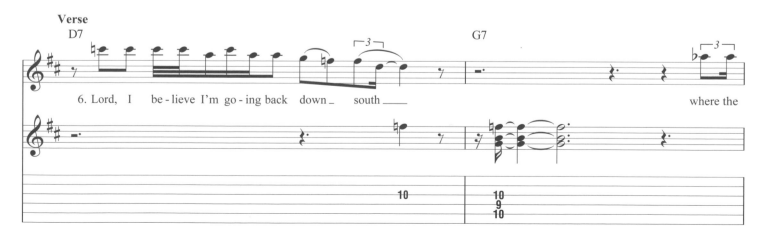

6. Lord, I be-lieve I'm go-ing back down _ south _____ where the

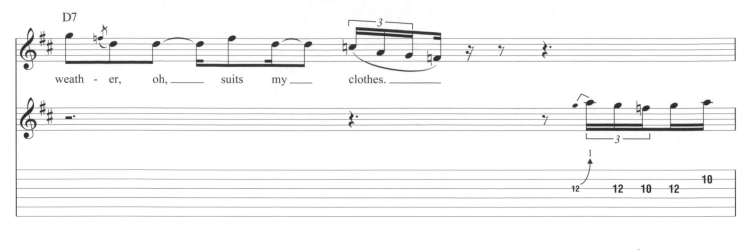

weath - er, oh, _____ suits my _____ clothes. _____

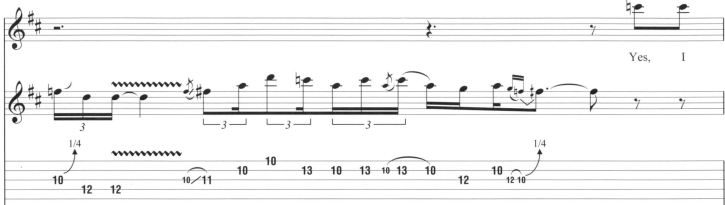

Yes, I

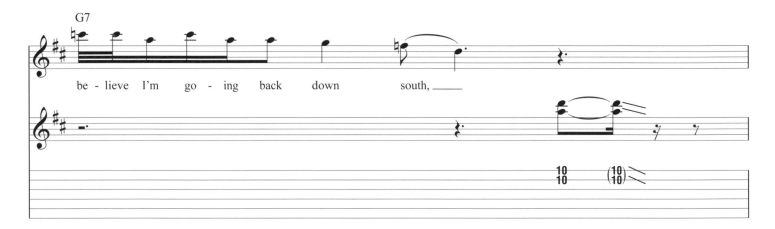

be - lieve I'm go - ing back down south, _____

Gtr. tacet

peo - ple, where the weath - er _____ suits my _____ clothes. _____

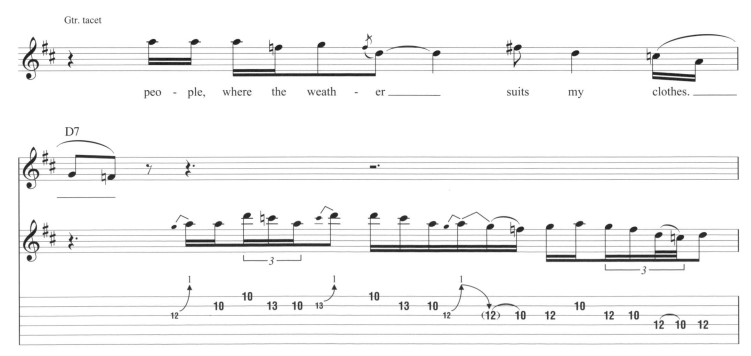

Yes, you know that ___

___ I've played a - round in these big cit - ies so long, ___ man, ___ ah,

oo, ___ till I ___ al - most done ___

froze. ___

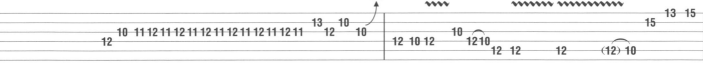

Begin fade *Fade out*

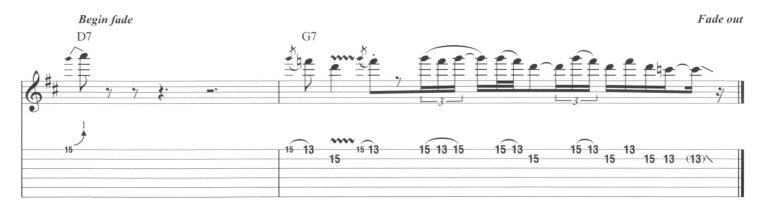

What Kind of Woman Is This

Words and Music by Buddy Guy

Intro
Moderately slow ♩ = 93

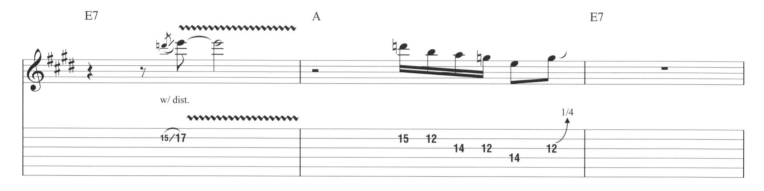

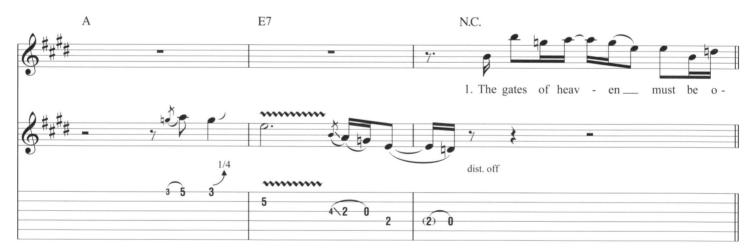

1. The gates of heav - en __ must be o-

Verse

pen.   I think I saw an an - gel   just walk by. __

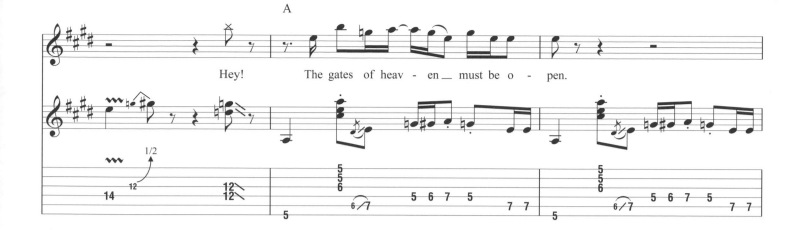

Hey! The gates of heav - en __ must be o - pen.

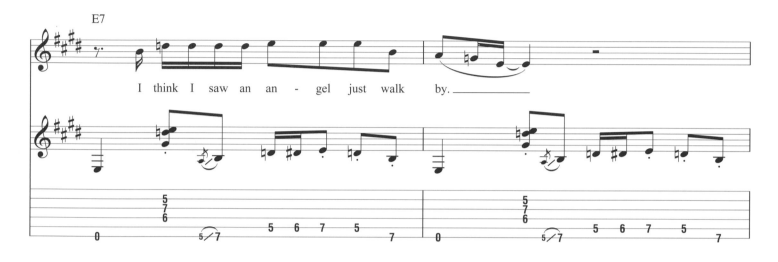

I think I saw an an - gel just walk by. _____

I heard __ a blind man scream and __ say, "Now there goes a sight for __ my sore

eyes." _____ There goes a sight for __ my sore __

bed - room _____ with me. _____ Oh, _____

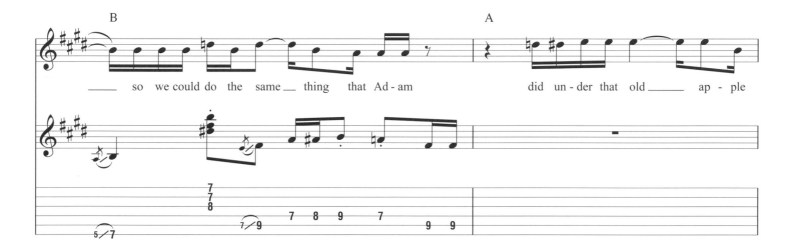

_____ so we could do the same _____ thing that Ad - am did un - der that old _____ ap - ple

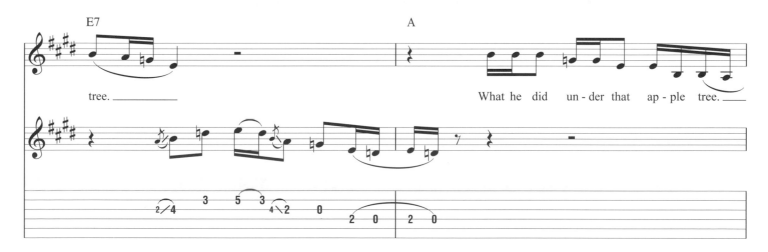

tree. _____ What he did un - der that ap - ple tree. _____

What he did _____ un - der that ap - ple tree. _____

Well, __ well, well, well, __ well,

well. _____

Look out!

Guitar Solo

*2nd string caught under bend finger.

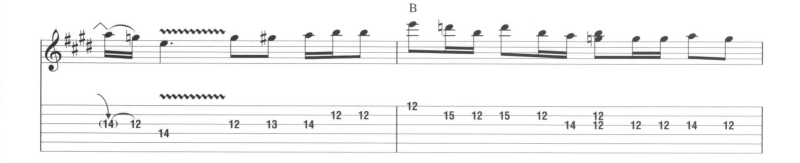

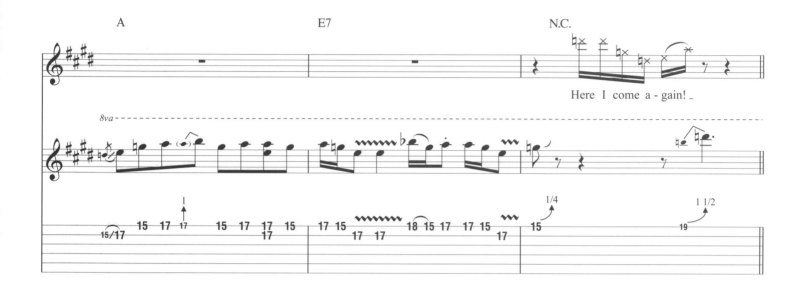

Here I come a - gain! _

Guitar Solo

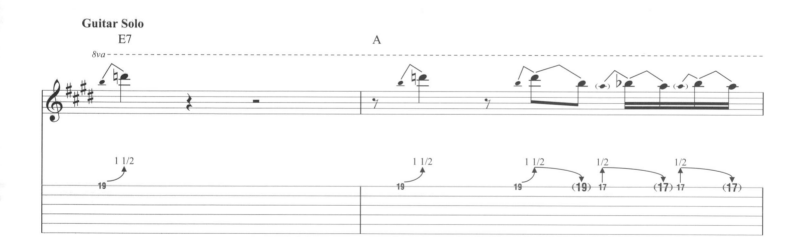

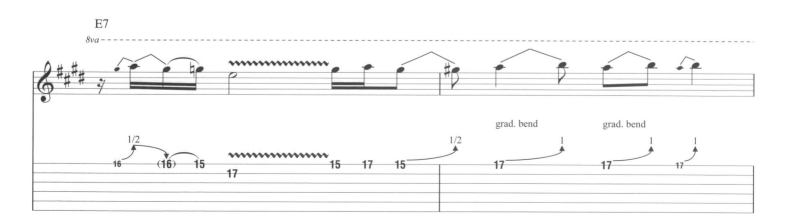

grad. bend   grad. bend

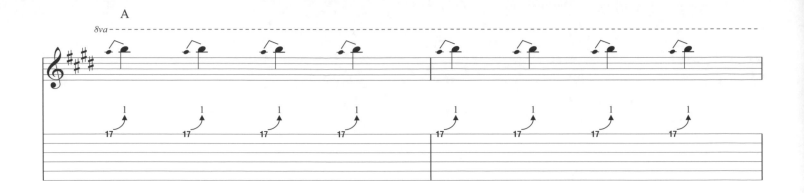

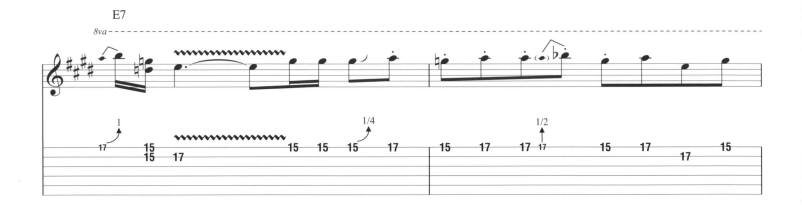

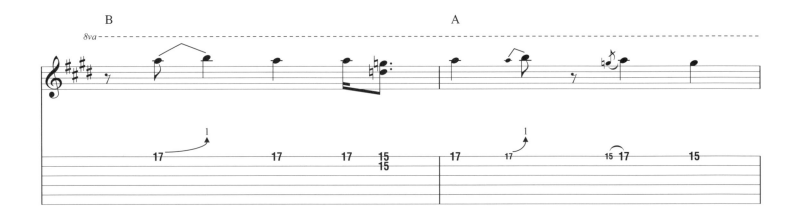

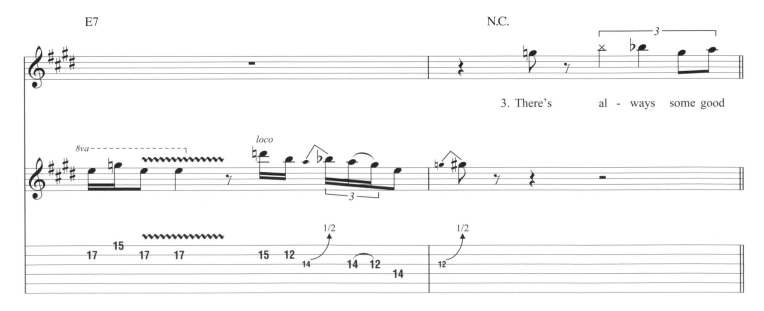

3. There's al - ways some good

Outro

made a dumb man _ talk. _   Oh.   What

kind of wom-an is this? _   Mm, _____

mm. _____   Sh - shucks.

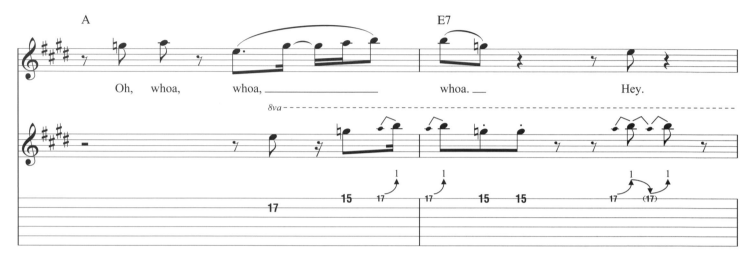

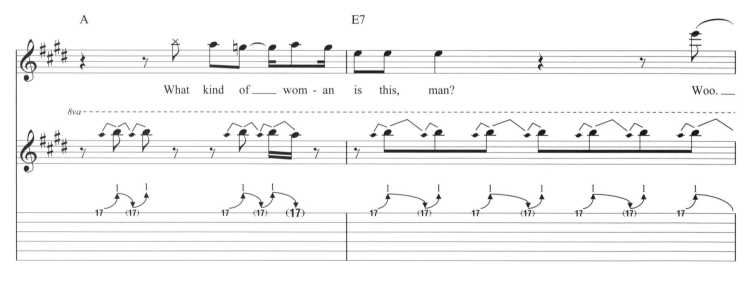

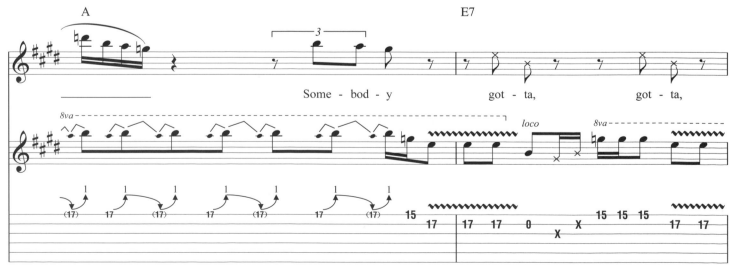

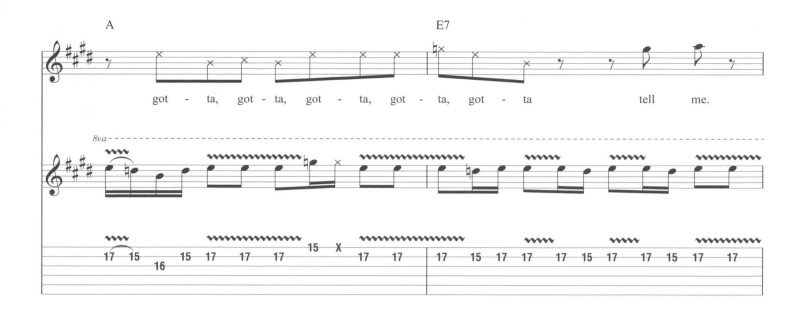

got - ta, got - ta, got - ta, got - ta, got - ta   tell   me.

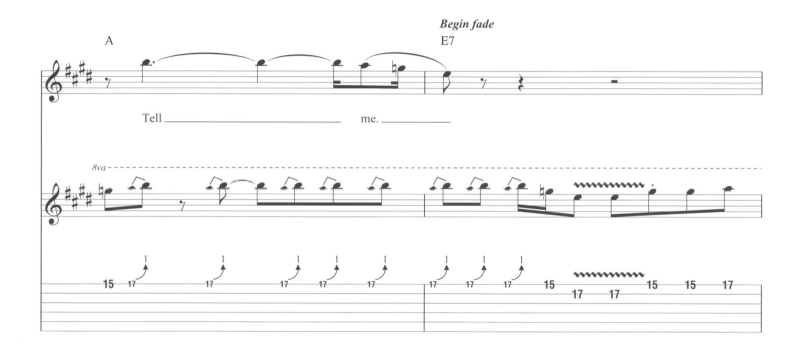

Tell _____ me. _____

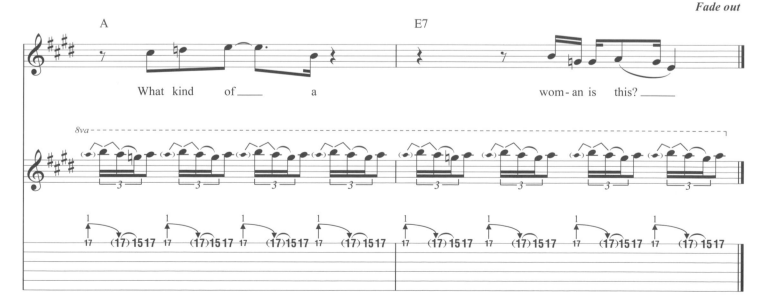

What kind of ____ a   wom - an is   this? _____

HAL•LEONARD GUITAR PLAY•ALONG

This series will help you play your favorite songs quickly and easily. Just follow the tab and listen to the audio to the hear how the guitar should sound, and then play along using the separate backing tracks. Mac or PC users can also slow down the tempo without changing pitch by using the CD in their computer. The melody and lyrics are included in the book so that you can sing or simply follow along.

INCLUDES TAB

VOL. 1 – ROCK	00699570 / $16.99
VOL. 2 – ACOUSTIC	00699569 / $16.95
VOL. 3 – HARD ROCK	00699573 / $16.95
VOL. 4 – POP/ROCK	00699571 / $16.99
VOL. 5 – MODERN ROCK	00699574 / $16.99
VOL. 6 – '90S ROCK	00699572 / $16.99
VOL. 7 – BLUES	00699575 / $16.95
VOL. 8 – ROCK	00699585 / $14.99
VOL. 10 – ACOUSTIC	00699586 / $16.95
VOL. 11 – EARLY ROCK	00699579 / $14.95
VOL. 12 – POP/ROCK	00699587 / $14.95
VOL. 13 – FOLK ROCK	00699581 / $15.99
VOL. 14 – BLUES ROCK	00699582 / $16.95
VOL. 15 – R&B	00699583 / $14.95
VOL. 16 – JAZZ	00699584 / $15.95
VOL. 17 – COUNTRY	00699588 / $15.95
VOL. 18 – ACOUSTIC ROCK	00699577 / $15.95
VOL. 19 – SOUL	00699578 / $14.99
VOL. 20 – ROCKABILLY	00699580 / $14.95
VOL. 21 – YULETIDE	00699602 / $14.95
VOL. 22 – CHRISTMAS	00699600 / $15.95
VOL. 23 – SURF	00699635 / $14.95
VOL. 24 – ERIC CLAPTON	00699649 / $17.99
VOL. 25 – LENNON & MCCARTNEY	00699642 / $16.99
VOL. 26 – ELVIS PRESLEY	00699643 / $14.95
VOL. 27 – DAVID LEE ROTH	00699645 / $16.95
VOL. 28 – GREG KOCH	00699646 / $14.95
VOL. 29 – BOB SEGER	00699647 / $15.99
VOL. 30 – KISS	00699644 / $16.99
VOL. 31 – CHRISTMAS HITS	00699652 / $14.95
VOL. 32 – THE OFFSPRING	00699653 / $14.95
VOL. 33 – ACOUSTIC CLASSICS	00699656 / $16.95
VOL. 34 – CLASSIC ROCK	00699658 / $16.95
VOL. 35 – HAIR METAL	00699660 / $16.95
VOL. 36 – SOUTHERN ROCK	00699661 / $16.95
VOL. 37 – ACOUSTIC UNPLUGGED	00699662 / $22.99
VOL. 38 – BLUES	00699663 / $16.95
VOL. 39 – '80S METAL	00699664 / $16.99
VOL. 40 – INCUBUS	00699668 / $17.95
VOL. 41 – ERIC CLAPTON	00699669 / $16.95
VOL. 42 – 2000S ROCK	00699670 / $16.99
VOL. 43 – LYNYRD SKYNYRD	00699681 / $17.95
VOL. 44 – JAZZ	00699689 / $14.99
VOL. 45 – TV THEMES	00699718 / $14.95
VOL. 46 – MAINSTREAM ROCK	00699722 / $16.95
VOL. 47 – HENDRIX SMASH HITS	00699723 / $19.95
VOL. 48 – AEROSMITH CLASSICS	00699724 / $17.99
VOL. 49 – STEVIE RAY VAUGHAN	00699725 / $17.99
VOL. 50 – VAN HALEN 1978-1984	00110269 / $17.99
VOL. 51 – ALTERNATIVE '90S	00699727 / $14.99
VOL. 52 – FUNK	00699728 / $14.95
VOL. 53 – DISCO	00699729 / $14.99
VOL. 54 – HEAVY METAL	00699730 / $14.95
VOL. 55 – POP METAL	00699731 / $14.95
VOL. 56 – FOO FIGHTERS	00699749 / $15.99
VOL. 57 – SYSTEM OF A DOWN	00699751 / $14.95
VOL. 58 – BLINK-182	00699772 / $14.95
VOL. 59 – CHET ATKINS	00702347 / $16.99
VOL. 60 – 3 DOORS DOWN	00699774 / $14.95
VOL. 61 – SLIPKNOT	00699775 / $16.99
VOL. 62 – CHRISTMAS CAROLS	00699798 / $12.95

VOL. 63 – CREEDENCE CLEARWATER REVIVAL	00699802 / $16.99
VOL. 64 – THE ULTIMATE OZZY OSBOURNE	00699803 / $16.99
VOL. 66 – THE ROLLING STONES	00699807 / $16.95
VOL. 67 – BLACK SABBATH	00699808 / $16.99
VOL. 68 – PINK FLOYD – DARK SIDE OF THE MOON	00699809 / $16.99
VOL. 69 – ACOUSTIC FAVORITES	00699810 / $14.95
VOL. 70 – OZZY OSBOURNE	00699805 / $16.99
VOL. 71 – CHRISTIAN ROCK	00699824 / $14.95
VOL. 73 – BLUESY ROCK	00699829 / $16.99
VOL. 75 – TOM PETTY	00699882 / $16.99
VOL. 76 – COUNTRY HITS	00699884 / $14.95
VOL. 77 – BLUEGRASS	00699910 / $14.99
VOL. 78 – NIRVANA	00700132 / $16.99
VOL. 79 – NEIL YOUNG	00700133 / $24.99
VOL. 80 – ACOUSTIC ANTHOLOGY	00700175 / $19.95
VOL. 81 – ROCK ANTHOLOGY	00700176 / $22.99
VOL. 82 – EASY SONGS	00700177 / $12.99
VOL. 83 – THREE CHORD SONGS	00700178 / $16.99
VOL. 84 – STEELY DAN	00700200 / $16.99
VOL. 85 – THE POLICE	00700269 / $16.99
VOL. 86 – BOSTON	00700465 / $16.99
VOL. 87 – ACOUSTIC WOMEN	00700763 / $14.99
VOL. 88 – GRUNGE	00700467 / $16.99
VOL. 89 – REGGAE	00700468 / $15.99
VOL. 90 – CLASSICAL POP	00700469 / $14.99
VOL. 91 – BLUES INSTRUMENTALS	00700505 / $14.99
VOL. 92 – EARLY ROCK INSTRUMENTALS	00700506 / $14.99
VOL. 93 – ROCK INSTRUMENTALS	00700507 / $16.99
VOL. 94 – SLOW BLUES	00700508 / $16.99
VOL. 95 – BLUES CLASSICS	00700509 / $14.99
VOL. 96 – THIRD DAY	00700560 / $14.95
VOL. 97 – ROCK BAND	00700703 / $14.99
VOL. 99 – ZZ TOP	00700762 / $16.99
VOL. 100 – B.B. KING	00700466 / $16.99
VOL. 101 – SONGS FOR BEGINNERS	00701917 / $14.99
VOL. 102 – CLASSIC PUNK	00700769 / $14.99
VOL. 103 – SWITCHFOOT	00700773 / $16.99
VOL. 104 – DUANE ALLMAN	00700846 / $16.99
VOL. 105 – LATIN	00700939 / $16.99
VOL. 106 – WEEZER	00700958 / $14.99
VOL. 107 – CREAM	00701069 / $16.99
VOL. 108 – THE WHO	00701053 / $16.99
VOL. 109 – STEVE MILLER	00701054 / $14.99
VOL. 110 – SLIDE GUITAR HITS	00701055 / $16.99
VOL. 111 – JOHN MELLENCAMP	00701056 / $14.99
VOL. 112 – QUEEN	00701052 / $16.99
VOL. 113 – JIM CROCE	00701058 / $15.99
VOL. 114 – BON JOVI	00701060 / $14.99
VOL. 115 – JOHNNY CASH	00701070 / $16.99
VOL. 116 – THE VENTURES	00701124 / $14.99
VOL. 117 – BRAD PAISLEY	00701224 / $16.99
VOL. 118 – ERIC JOHNSON	00701353 / $16.99
VOL. 119 – AC/DC CLASSICS	00701356 / $17.99
VOL. 120 – PROGRESSIVE ROCK	00701457 / $14.99
VOL. 121 – U2	00701508 / $16.99
VOL. 122 – CROSBY, STILLS & NASH	00701610 / $16.99
VOL. 123 – LENNON & MCCARTNEY ACOUSTIC	00701614 / $16.99
VOL. 125 – JEFF BECK	00701687 / $16.99

VOL. 126 – BOB MARLEY	00701701 / $16.99
VOL. 127 – 1970S ROCK	00701739 / $14.99
VOL. 128 – 1960S ROCK	00701740 / $14.99
VOL. 129 – MEGADETH	00701741 / $16.99
VOL. 131 – 1990S ROCK	00701743 / $14.99
VOL. 132 – COUNTRY ROCK	00701757 / $15.99
VOL. 133 – TAYLOR SWIFT	00701894 / $16.99
VOL. 134 – AVENGED SEVENFOLD	00701906 / $16.99
VOL. 136 – GUITAR THEMES	00701922 / $14.99
VOL. 137 – IRISH TUNES	00701966 / $15.99
VOL. 138 – BLUEGRASS CLASSICS	00701967 / $14.99
VOL. 139 – GARY MOORE	00702370 / $16.99
VOL. 140 – MORE STEVIE RAY VAUGHAN	00702396 / $17.99
VOL. 141 – ACOUSTIC HITS	00702401 / $16.99
VOL. 143 – SLASH	00702425 / $19.99
VOL. 144 – DJANGO REINHARDT	00702531 / $16.99
VOL. 145 – DEF LEPPARD	00702532 / $16.99
VOL. 146 – ROBERT JOHNSON	00702533 / $16.99
VOL. 147 – SIMON & GARFUNKEL	14041591 / $16.99
VOL. 148 – BOB DYLAN	14041592 / $16.99
VOL. 149 – AC/DC HITS	14041593 / $17.99
VOL. 150 – ZAKK WYLDE	02501717 / $16.99
VOL. 152 – JOE BONAMASSA	02501751 / $19.99
VOL. 153 – RED HOT CHILI PEPPERS	00702990 / $19.99
VOL. 155 – ERIC CLAPTON – FROM THE ALBUM UNPLUGGED	00703085 / $16.99
VOL. 156 – SLAYER	00703770 / $17.99
VOL. 157 – FLEETWOOD MAC	00101382 / $16.99
VOL. 158 – ULTIMATE CHRISTMAS	00101889 / $14.99
VOL. 159 – WES MONTGOMERY	00102593 / $19.99
VOL. 160 – T-BONE WALKER	00102641 / $16.99
VOL. 161 – THE EAGLES – ACOUSTIC	00102659 / $17.99
VOL. 162 – THE EAGLES HITS	00102667 / $17.99
VOL. 163 – PANTERA	00103036 / $17.99
VOL. 164 – VAN HALEN 1986-1995	00110270 / $17.99
VOL. 166 – MODERN BLUES	00700764 / $16.99
VOL. 168 – KISS	00113421 / $16.99
VOL. 169 – TAYLOR SWIFT	00115982 / $16.99
VOL. 170 – THREE DAYS GRACE	00117337 / $16.99
VOL. 171 – JAMES BROWN	00117420 / $16.99
VOL. 172 – THE DOOBIE BROTHERS	00119670 / $16.99
VOL. 174 – SCORPIONS	00122119 / $16.99
VOL. 175 – MICHAEL SCHENKER	00122127 / $16.99
VOL. 176 – BLUES BREAKERS WITH JOHN MAYALL & ERIC CLAPTON	00122132 / $19.99
VOL. 177 – ALBERT KING	00123271 / $16.99
VOL. 178 – JASON MRAZ	00124165 / $17.99
VOL. 179 – RAMONES	00127073 / $16.99
VOL. 180 – BRUNO MARS	00129706 / $16.99
VOL. 181 – JACK JOHNSON	00129854 / $16.99
VOL. 182 – SOUNDGARDEN	00138161 / $17.99
VOL. 184 – KENNY WAYNE SHEPHERD	00138258 / $17.99
VOL. 187 – JOHN DENVER	00140839 / $17.99

Complete song lists available online.

Prices, contents, and availability subject to change without notice.

HAL•LEONARD CORPORATION

7777 W. BLUEMOUND RD. P.O. BOX 13819 MILWAUKEE, WI 53213

www.halleonard.com